THE MAJOR WORKS OF
H. G. WELLS

THE TIME MACHINE
THE INVISIBLE MAN
THE WAR OF THE WORLDS
TONO-BUNGAY

RANDALL H. KEENAN
DEPARTMENT OF ENGLISH
NASSAU COMMUNITY COLLEGE

MONARCH
PRESS

Published by
MONARCH PRESS
a Simon & Schuster division of
Gulf & Western Corporation
Simon & Schuster Building
1230 Avenue of the Americas
New York, N.Y. 10020

Standard Book Number: 0-671-00766-1

Library of Congress Catalog Card Number: 65-56929

MONARCH PRESS and colophon are trademarks of Simon & Schuster, registered in the U.S. Patent and Trademark Office.

Printed in the United States of America

CONTENTS

Human history becomes more and more a race between education and catastrophe.

(H. G. Wells: The Outline of History)

CHRONOLOGY

1886   Born in Bromley, Kent, England, September 21, to Joseph and Sarah (Neal) Wells.

1880   Apprenticed to a draper.

1888   B.S. degree, first-class honors from University of London.

1891   Marries his cousin Isabel.

1893   Leaves wife to live with and later marry Amy Catherine Robbins, nicknamed "Jane," who bears him two sons.

1895   *The Time Machine: An Invention* (Science Fiction)

1896   *The Island of Doctor Moreau* (Science Fiction)

1897   *The Invisible Man: A Grotesque Romance* (Science Fiction)

1898   *The War of the Worlds* (Science Fiction)

1901   *The First Men in the Moon* (Science Fiction)

1903   Joins the Socialist Fabian Society.

1905   *Kipps, The Story of a Simple Soul* (Novel)

1908   Disenchanted with Fabians and leaves the society.

1909   *Tono-Bungay* (Novel)

1910   *The History of Mr. Polly* (Novel)

1911   "The Contemporary Novel" (Essay)

        The Country of the Blind (Short Stories)

1919–20   *The Outline of History*, 2 vols.

1926   *The World of William Clissold*, 3 vols. (Novel)

1929–30   *The Science of Life* (Biology). Written with his son G. P. Wells and Julian Huxley.

1933 *The Shape of Things To Come: The Ultimate Revolution* (Prophecy)

1934 *Experiment in Autobiography*

1941 *Guide to the New World Order* (Commentary)

1942 *The Outlook for Homo Sapiens* (Commentary)

1945 *Mind at the End of Its Tether* (Commentary)

1946 Died August 13, 1946, in London—one month before his eightieth birthday.

INTRODUCTION

THE EARLY YEARS: Henry George Wells was born September 21, 1866, in Bromley, Kent, England. In the third quarter of the nineteenth century Bromley still retained its status as a small country town, and it was here that Joseph and Sarah Neal Wells, lower middle class socially, maintained a crockery and china shop that also carried a small stock of cricket equipment. This latter is explainable by the fact that Joseph Wells was a professional cricketeer in Kent. He was well known as a player and instructor, and this produced a small income to be added to the already meager sums realized from the crockery business at 47 High Street. The Wellses were anything but well-to-do. With this in mind Sarah Wells attended to her three sons' futures by seeing to it that they were placed as apprentices in the drapery business. However, there was one mitigating circumstance. The elder Wells had been encouraged to read widely by one of his employers and this he passed on to young George. Their home had a variety of books and the imaginative seed was well sown. The year 1881 found H. G. Wells serving as a chemist's assistant in Midhurst, a fact which entered autobiographically into *Tono-Bungay*, one of the novels to be examined in this guide. An apprenticeship in a more substantial draper's establishment proved unsatisfactory for the young Wells; and in 1883, prompted by dissatisfaction, he walked seventeen miles to Hampshire to meet his mother on her return from Sunday church. At that time Mrs. Wells was employed as a housekeeper at Up Park, a great mansion near Petersfield in Hampshire. Joseph Wells had remained at Bromley. In *Tono-Bungay* we shall see young George Ponderevo walk miles to encounter his mother returning from church. The fictional Mrs. Ponderevo is a housekeeper at Bladesover, an eighteenth-century home of manorial splendor and the literary counterpart for Up Park, Sarah Wells's place of domestic employment. Wells's flight from his draper's apprenticeship had a cause additional to that of boredom. He had better things in view; namely, those offered by the headmaster of the Midhurst Grammar School, who had tutored him in Latin during his service as a chemist's assistant in the town. He was engaged as a pupil teacher, and he was now on his way up and beyond the social class to which he had been born. When he had taken examinations and won grants, Wells was brought to London by the Ministry of Education and there provided with three years of tuition-free education. In 1888 Wells received a B.Sc. degree with first-class honors from the University of London.

THE SCIENTIFIC ROMANCES: Between 1895 and 1908, Wells produced the bulk of his splendid "scientific romances," as he called them. These were narratives of the future, startling and visionary for readers who could accept space travel only as entertaining fantasy, and who would not see the Wright brothers get their flying machine aloft until 1903. But Wells always looked toward the future and longed in a utopian way for moral, economic and ethical improvement along socialistic lines. Even in such science fiction of the nineties as *The Time Machine* (1895) and *The War of the Worlds* (1898), there are repeated references and echoes of Wells's preoccupation with what he saw as a diseased society, grim in outlook if insufficiencies were not corrected. The "scientific romances," however, are amazingly prophetic and indicate how Wells's scientific training blended with a fertile imagination to create fantastic material that is no longer that outlandish. The idea of time travel is certainly not a reality today, but the notion of time as a fourth dimension has been explored theoretically by Albert Einstein. Its staggering proportions are at least being examined. In *The War of the Worlds,* there is space travel, to be sure; but there are also the forerunners of poison gas warfare and the laserlike Heat-Ray. Wells's untethered scientific vision has, indeed, become a more creditable thing as the decades have passed.

THE SOCIAL COMMENTATOR: Somehow, in Wells, there is a common meeting ground for the scientist and the speculative philosopher; his severe criticisms of society doom prophetically and yet simultaneously offer a distant way ahead leading to a socialistic salvation. In 1903 Wells joined the Fabians, a socialist movement, one of whose members was the playwright George Bernard Shaw. But Wells found the Fabians too slow for his impatient and aggressive One-World State socialist spirit, and so in 1908 he broke with the group. In *Tono-Bungay* we shall see evidence of his disenchantment with them. Wells was, indeed, correct in his awareness that society was in a process of change. Victorianism with its restrictions, its patterns, and its built-in negation of change was on the wane. The mid-Victorians had the foundations of biblical beliefs and its notions on the evolution of man, severely damaged by Darwin's *The Origin of the Species by Means of Natural Selection* (1859). In his student days, Wells had come in contact for a time with Thomas Henry Huxley, the foremost exponent of Darwinism, and was influenced by him. But there was an evolutionary process in society also for Wells. What was this new century to offer? Were the old neo-feudal responses to humanity and society to remain? Wells hoped it would not be so and was anxious for the new socialistic order to materialize. He had hoped that the Fabians might be employed as a training establishment for a socialistic elite, but the Fabians were not dedicated to a violent and militant response to capitalism. To Shaw and the Fabians, then, such a proposal was an outlandish thing.

With the conclusion of World War I, Wells enthusiastically espoused the plan for establishing a League of Nations. But the League was not to be the beginning of a world government, a notion that was dear to Wells's thinking. The League was not Wellsian and brought with it as much disillusionment for Wells as the Fabians had brought. In 1919–20 Wells took things in hand and produced his own history of the world: *The Outline of History* in two volumes. By the year 1932 he had produced two closely related works: *The Science of Life* and *The Work, Wealth, and Happiness of Mankind* which, when added to *The Outline of History,* represented a stunning achievement. Yet, *The Outline* cannot go unchallenged, regardless of the range it encompasses. More Wellsian than objective, it has more than a legitimate personal bias in its preparation. It is Wells without doubt, and so as an historical document it contains more than an acceptable personal coloring of fact.

SOCIAL CRITIC AND AUTOBIOGRAPHER: The reader who engages even a limited amount of H. G. Wells's great body of writing cannot avoid the intrinsic vein of frustration present there. Certainly, his literary efforts were not idle exercises. He wished to be literarily entertaining, but the didactic social crusader made his presence known almost unceasingly.

In addition, much of what Wells transferred to the reader of social criticism and literary creation was remarkably autobiographical. His first marriage to his cousin was unsuccessful and resulted in divorce when he went to live with a biology student, Amy Robbins. Eventually he legitimatized this relationship but, incredibly, came to a point where he asked his second wife to approve of his promiscuity. Wells's personal attitudes toward marriage materialize in his literary efforts, and as readers we are forced to distinguish between his legitimate efforts at social improvement and frequent extensions of personal enigmas. Wells's sense of frustration had considerable latitude. In addition, his early life as a draper's apprentice and his struggle for a legitimate education materialize forcefully in his work, and when we encounter *Tono-Bungay,* the autobiographical Wells will manifest himself strikingly.

INCREDIBLE PROPHECY: Of all Wells's fantastic prophecies, the foreshadowing of the atomic age is by far the most profound. In *Tono-Bungay,* through the character of George Ponderevo, Wells speculates on the eventual demise of mankind's achievements through atomic decay.

Stunningly contemporary to be sure, but later, in 1914, in his fantasy *A World Set Free,* Wells comments:

> Nothing could have been more obvious to the people of the early twentieth century than the rapidity with which war was becoming impossible. And as certainly they did not see it. They did not see it until the atomic bombs burst in their fumbling hands.

In the same work Wells observed with incredible contemporary significance:

> The catastrophe of the atomic bombs which shook men out of cities and businesses and economic relations, shook them also out of their old established habits of thought, and out of the lightly held beliefs and prejudices that came down to them from the past.

The above quotations require little comment; their significance and their contemporary force is manifest. It is all too obvious that Wells's prognostications were unbelievably frightening in their accuracy. His turn-of-the-century apprehensions have become the legitimate fears of mid-twentieth-century humanity. Atomic warfare and its aftermath is the reality that H. G. Wells foresaw even at the brink of World War I. He was, in fact, a prophet of doom.

WELLS TODAY: There is no doubt that Wells's theories and prophecies have come a long way towards realization since the days of Edwardian England. Yet, a statement such as this seems purposely to ignore the work of the man until his death in 1946. The truth cannot be ignored, however: Wells's influence and significance as a literary figure deteriorated as his zeal for social reformation increased. There is no doubt that in his case the socialist cause was an unfortunate companion for the novelist. Henry James remarked that Wells had a "robust pitch" of style, and that his literary "eye" and "ear" would have turned even Charles Dickens to envy. An examination of *Tono-Bungay* makes this observation valid. It is unfortunate, however, that Wells's later work departed from the novelist's commitment; for with the latter part of his life, his influence along with his literary imprint upon the world faded considerably. Henry George Wells was not a great thinker. He was a marvelously realistic and imaginative writer, whose vision has proven remarkably accurate during the first seven decades of the twentieth century. He was a man who longed passionately for a better world, and this in itself is good. He was a man between ages, between the staid repressiveness of Victorian England and the hopeful expanses of the new century. His work is good literature to be sure; Wells's narrative power can never be denied. Moreover, he had an impatient social voice, not entirely acceptable, but one that yearned for the betterment of mankind and hopefully anticipated the balance of man's desires with his undeniable needs.

THE TIME MACHINE

CHAPTER 1

There had been a small dinner party and it was that moment when relaxation and good conversation take hold. In the course of conversation, the host, identified only as the Time Traveller, had suggested that much of the geometry commonly taught in the schools is basically erroneous. A gentleman named Filby and a psychologist objected to this but the Time Traveller was most convincing. He observed that any real body must possess extension in four directions; there must be length, breadth, thickness and duration. This last element is one of time, and people habitually ignore it in relation to the other three because human consciousness moves along a belt of time throughout life. With the encouragement of a provincial mayor present at the dinner party, the Time Traveller proceeded with his consideration of the dimension of time, the Fourth Dimension, as he referred to it. Some scientists, he added, believe it possible to draw a four dimensional figure on a flat surface—if only the particular perspective could be handled properly. Several pictures of a man made at different ages in his life would be three dimensional yet would present a dimension of time, the fourth-dimensional aspect of the man. The Time Traveller observed that time is only a kind of fourth dimension of space, and this drew an objection from a medical man present, who wondered why then it is not possible to move as freely in time as we do in space. But space too limits man, replied the Time Traveller; does not the force of gravity act upon us? The psychologist observed that man, however, cannot move about in time at all. Wrong, replied the host, for movement in time is at the heart of his wonderful new discovery. After all, man can defy the force of gravity, and so why should he not be able to regulate his passage along the dimension of time, moving ahead or even back along its path?

The Time Traveller's guests were rather amused by his theories, and an unidentified young man who was present remarked facetiously that a man might make investments in the present and then hustle along into the future to collect the interest. But then, responded the narrator, one might land in a communistic future.

The guests then demanded some experimental proof for their host's wild theories about travel through time. The Time Traveller smiled, left the room, and returned shortly with a small metal framework with some ivory and transparent crystalline parts, intricately assembled and barely larger than a small clock. The host placed the device on a nearby table he had drawn before the fire, and his guests gathered closely about it. Everyone watched carefully, and it appeared to the narrator that any sleight-of-hand or bold effort at deception would not explain what occurred shortly thereafter. The Time Traveller explained that it had taken two years to construct the model mechanism and indicated the various parts such as two white levers, a seat in which a time traveller could sit, and a curious little bar that seemed to twinkle. One lever propels the machine into the future, explained the host, and the other simply reverses the process. After emphasizing that there was no trickery involved, the host requested that the psychologist be the one to move one of the levers and send the little machine into the dimension of time. As the psychologist moved the lever, the narrator was convinced that there was no trickery involved on the part of the host. There was a quick gust of wind, a candle blew out, the lamp flame flickered, and after becoming indistinct and barely visible, the model time machine vanished. The guests were stunned but, nevertheless, wondered soberly if the host really expected them to believe that the little device had traveled through time. I do, indeed, said the Time Traveller, and after some discussion about whether the machine had gone into the future or the past, he explained that while the machine had moved through time and not space, it was not visible since it passed through large portions of time in only a second, thus diluting or thinning out its appearance at any one moment. Believable now, said the medical man, but he wondered how common sense would treat the matter the next day.

The Time Traveller then offered to show his guests the full-sized machine he was constructing and led them to his laboratory. There it stood, an enlarged version of the device that had disappeared before their eyes a few minutes before. The narrator observed that there were nickel, ivory and rock crystal parts to it, and that the two bars or levers for the device lay unfinished on a workbench. He handled them carefully and noticed that they seemed to be made of quartz.

The medical man questioned the seriousness of the whole business and the Time Traveller was emphatic in his claim that he intended positively to explore time. No one knew quite what to say, but the narrator noticed Filby toss him a rather knowing wink.

COMMENT: After one of their frequent dinners together, several educated and sophisticated English gentlemen are presented with an incredible demonstration and an even more incredible concept: time travel. The demonstration has been made. The eyes have seen, but the mind boggles and falls back upon skepticism in the face of the unreasonable, declining to accept what experience and training tell them is impossible. Yet, how credible Wells makes his fiction at the very outset! So much that the Time Traveller's explanations and theories tend to convince the reader whether or not they persuade the Traveller's guests. In our own time much of what was once science fiction is now vivid reality, and we have in many ways become accustomed to the surprises that science presents with amazing frequency. But how startling and excitingly persuasive must have been *The Time Machine* when H. G. Wells published it near the very end of Victorian era, the beauty and terror of time travel told through the reminiscence of a narrator to an audience who read by gaslights and awaited the beginning of the twentieth century.

CHAPTER 2

The Time Traveller was an extremely clever man, but somewhat whimsical, and so it was difficult not to believe that he had brought off some splendid illusion in this matter of the time machine and time travel. However, on the following Thursday the narrator went once again to the Time Traveller's home in Richmond for the customary dinner party. Arriving late he discovered the psychologist, the doctor, an editor named Blank, and a quiet, bearded gentleman already present. Their host had said that he would be late for dinner and that the group should begin without him. The narrator had just suggested humorously that his absence might be due to time travel when the host himself entered the room. The guests stood amazed at what they saw, for the Time Traveller was a ragged sight. His coat was dirty and stained with green along the sleeves. He was pale with disheveled hair somewhat grayer than the narrator remembered it, and there was a partially healed cut on his chin. The Traveller excused himself to wash and dress, and as he left the room the narrator observed that he limped and wore only torn and blood-soaked socks upon his feet. In his absence the journalist and the editor, in a jesting and irreverent fashion, ridiculed the notion of time travel as an explanation for their host's tattered appearance. However, the narrator caught the glance of the psychologist and each confirmed the other's suspicion that a trip through time might be nearer the truth.

When the host returned he seated himself at the table and asked for a piece of mutton. It was good to taste meat again, he said, and would not expand upon his appearance other than to confirm that he had traveled through time. He ate vigorously, drank wine, and at the end of the uneasy meal, lit a cigar and suggested that they all retire to the smoking room where he would explain his incredible adventure. He was very eager to recount what had happened but he would not debate the circumstances and did not wish to be interrupted in his telling. He had lived through eight days since he went into his laboratory at four o'clock that very day. What he would now narrate might seem like falsehood and fantasy; however, it was true.

COMMENT: The dramatic entrance of the Time Traveller, shabby and bruised, foreshadows the nightmarish adventure he is about to relate. His appearance and actions are not haphazardly contrived by Wells, and reasons for the half-healed cut on his chin, the craving for meat, the green smears down his sleeves and his pronounced limp will become evident as the book progresses.

CHAPTER 3

The Time Traveller began his story and pointed to the Time Machine, with one of its ivory bars cracked and a brass rail twisted out of shape, the results of his curious adventure. It was not until ten o'clock that very morning that the machine was completed and ready for testing, and the Traveller confessed that he felt like a man contemplating suicide, sitting in the saddle of the machine with his hands clutching the starting and stopping levers. He pressed the forward lever and then immediately followed with the stop. He trembled, seemed to be falling, and presumed that nothing had really happened until he noticed that the clock now said almost three-thirty when the hands had stood at almost ten o'clock a moment before. He then steadied himself, gripped the start lever, and was off on a journey into time. Night and day suddenly fell upon one another in dizzying repetition, the laboratory blurred from view, a swirl of sound filled his ears and the Time Traveller's mind spun about in helpless confusion. The sensations were extremely unpleasant, he confessed, and he was certain of crashing momentarily. He accelerated and day and night flew past in a wild blinking which pained his eyes considerably. The sun bounded across the heavens. The moon hurtled through its quarters and gradually the sky became a deep blue. The sun was a golden arch, the moon a pale ribbon above him. On the hillside where his house and laboratory had been, the landscape was indistinct, but he was conscious of trees and buildings rising and falling in an instant. The world appeared to flow through its seasonal changes, and soon he was aware that his speed had reached a year a minute. A wild giddiness replaced the discomfort he experienced at first, and he raced on into the future as the Time Machine swayed about eccentrically.

With a mixture of curiosity and apprehension, he contemplated the wonderful civilizations that might lie before him, and he began to think about coming to a stop. However, there was the problem of colliding with whatever object or substance occupied in the future the space which the Time Machine now held. There was, of course, the chance of obliteration. The risk would have to be taken, and in a rash of confused and nervous impatience the Traveller leaned hard upon the stop lever. The Time Machine lurched, careened over and amid the sound of thunder the Time Traveller was pitched out. When he regained his senses, he discovered himself sitting on a green lawn in what appeared to be a small park. It was hailing, and nearby he spied the overturned Time Machine. The hail had created a mist that shrouded everything in haziness. Nearby was a massive carved statue. It was fashioned of white marble and was sphinxlike, but with its wings spread out in a hovering position. It stood on a bronze pedestal now green with age. As a hint of sunlight began to appear overhead, the Time Traveller speculated on what man might have come to in this far extension of time. Had men been driven to total cruelty? Had they mutated into something insensitive and inhuman? Would they simply see him as a repulsive relic of a savage age and kill him without delay?

As the summer sky cleared to a bright blue, he distinguished huge buildings with parapets and towers. Facing the unknown, the Time Traveller suddenly became aware of the vulnerability of his position. What was apprehension quickly gave way to a fearful frenzy, and he wrestled with the machine in an effort to right it. As it swung upright, it smashed against his chin sharply. However, with his means of escape restored the Traveller regained his courage, and a calm curiosity gripped him. Suddenly, through the bushes by the winged statue, men came running. When one of them appeared at last, he was no more than four feet in height, clad in a purple tunic belted about the waist, and was wearing what seemed to be sandals. His legs were bare and he wore nothing upon his head. Standing in the unusually warm summer air, the Time Traveller saw that the little figure was both graceful and lovely, almost fragile in appearance, with a heightened and somewhat unhealthy color to his complexion. The Traveller suddenly became more relaxed.

COMMENT: For every minute that passes, the Time Traveller has passed through the equivalent of one year, and with his extraordinary speed night and day, summer and winter and the passing of civilizations have become nothing more than a blinking blur, much like a movie film speeded up beyond recognition. It should also be remembered that the Traveller is moving through time and not through space. When his machine finally comes to rest somewhere in the future, he is still on the spot where his home and laboratory were located in the past. He is still on the very spot in England on which he began, but that location is now in the future. Not distance but time has been covered in his journey; he has moved along what he had referred to as a fourth dimension.

Wells's wonderful scientific imagination includes a splendid and almost credible theoretical problem as the Time Traveller contemplates a landing. What if some object or building should now occupy the space where his laboratory once stood? What would occur as the atoms of the machine and those of the object attempt to occupy the same space? Fortunately, the problem resolved itself, but such practical considerations by Wells make the wildly fantastic appear almost plausible.

CHAPTER 4

The Time Traveller was startled when the small and lovely creature that stood before him looked into his eyes and laughed without a hint of fear. As a group of some eight or ten of these small creatures gathered about the Traveller, he noticed that they conversed in a sweet flowing language, totally unintelligible to him. In a gentle and childlike way, they began to touch him inquisitively. Soon they were examining the Time Machine and wisely the Traveller removed the two propelling levers and placed them in his pocket. These gentle beings stood about, smiling at him and conversing with one another in mild cooing sounds. There was little if any diversity in their appearance, and they all seemed to have curly hair, small thin mouths and pointed chins. Their lips were a vivid red, their eyes large and gentle, and their ears exceptionally small. Their skin was smooth and shiny as china, and there was no trace of hair to be seen on their faces.

In an effort to communicate with these curious people, the Time Traveller gestured towards the sun in an attempted reference to time. One of the creatures then imitated the sound of thunder. With this the Traveller was suddenly struck by the realization that he was being asked if he had come from the sun in a thunderstorm. Rather than superior intellects, these gentle creatures seemed to have the intelligence of five-year-olds. In a flood of despair the Time Traveller wondered if his great experiment had been all in vain. He again pointed to the sun and this time imitated a thunderclap, sending the small creatures scurrying in fright. Just as suddenly, however, they returned laughing and smiling happily and heaping strange and beautiful flowers upon their unexpected guest. The Time Traveller was then led to a huge building remarkable for its poor state of repair. On the way he noticed that the world now seemed to be a vast wild garden, uncared for, but luxuriant with magnificent flowers and bushes. He was brought to a great hall illuminated by light admitted through partially glazed windows. The floor was made of blocks of white metal and was much worn. The hall itself contained foot-high slabs of smooth stone like tables, and upon these were an abundance of strange fruits. The small creatures led their guest to cushions, and once seated, all began to devour the fruit. The Time Traveller observed that the large hall was shabby and damaged here and there; as he ate, the two hundred or so little people that ate with him sat and watched him with supreme interest. Fruit comprised their entire diet, for all warm-blooded edible animals had gone down to extinction through the ages. The Time Traveller then resolved to learn the strange cooing language of these people. He persisted and made some progress, but the little people quickly tired and lost interest. He admitted to himself that he had never encountered a more indolent or easily exhausted people anywhere. Their interest span was brief, and they were curious about him in the way that children are momentarily taken with a new toy.

When he left the hall, the Traveller decided to explore and determine just what the world looked like in the year Eight Hundred and Two Thousand Seven Hundred and One A.D. As he moved toward a hill some distance off, he was struck by the ruinous condition of everything about him. A great heap of granite and the ruins of walls lay before him; as he glanced about, he realized that no small houses were to be seen, only great palacelike structures here and there. Communism, he thought, and moved on. Several of the gentle little people had followed him, and it was now that he came to realize that there appeared to be no differences between the sexes. In the soft silklike togas they all wore and in all aspects of their appearance and bearing, they were alike. Even the children seemed but small replicas of the adults.

It seemed to the Traveller that the similarity between the sexes occurred naturally because these people lived securely and without fear. The unity of the family, the division of occupations therein, and the differing natures of the sexes would tend to even out in such a secure society, observed the Traveller, for they are necessities attendant only upon more forceful and insecure societies. Where balance, security and abundance prevail in the population, excessive childbearing and the need for a traditional family unit is undesirable for the state. Thus, speculated the Time Traveller, the contrasting roles performed by each sex relating to the children's needs tend to disappear. Soon enough, however, he would discover how wrong he was in his speculations about the peculiar little people.

As he moved up to the crest of the hill he soon left his band of admirers behind. While walking he was attracted by a curious well-like structure and thought it strange that wells had survived so long into the future. Once at the hilltop, he discovered a seat fashioned of some corroded yellow metal, sat down, and gazed out over the Thames valley upon what seemed one vast overgrown garden, here and there dotted with great palacelike buildings, cupolas and obelisks in various states of disrepair. Contemplating what he had seen so far in this world of the future, the Time Traveller began to speculate on the course humanity had taken. This certainly must be the sunset of mankind, he thought, the logical consequence of man's triumph over our environment; man's civilizing process that seeks to make life more secure must have proceeded steadily to a climax. Current dreams had become reality, and the ultimate result was what he saw before him. Disease had been vanquished, horticulture perfected; the whole world, intelligent, enlightened and joining in the ultimate victory over nature. Finally, animal and vegetable life had been balanced to complement human needs. Looking about him, the Time Traveller concluded that his speculations must be accurate. There seemed to be no disease among this strange people. Sweet fruits and beautiful flowers abounded without weeds or fungi, and the air was free of annoying insects. Certainly, this was a social paradise, for man was handsomely clothed and living in huge magnificent houses. There appeared to be no daily toil, no fierce social and economic competition. In short, the robustness and high pitch of commerce were absent. It seemed to be a golden age, one in which overpopulation had been solved with the population no longer increasing. With man's victory over his environment came the diminishing of hardship, of a yearning for freedom, and of driving human passions — those things that so discomfort us now. With these diminished or unnecessary, human intelligence and vigor would wane as well. It was a matter, no doubt, of the human conquest of nature followed by human adaptations to the change. Thus, our own restless drives which are strengths in our own age would be weaknesses and out of place in this future time. Even artistic energies had waned until these small creatures of the future were content to sing, dance and cover themselves with pretty flowers. Pain and necessity render us alert and prepared in our time, but here in this paradise the struggle is over. It was a grand theory the Time Traveller had evolved as he sat on the hilltop and contemplated the world about him — but unfortunately it was dead wrong.

COMMENT: In *Meanwhile* (1927), Wells spoke of "all this world of ours [as] nothing more than the prelude to a real civilization." The biographical portion of this guide has already commented on Wells's social consciousness, and here we discover him meditating on the evolution of man's civilized effort to control his environment. The abrasive elements have vanished and a type of delicate utopia has materialized. Man is secure and, with tensions and drives eliminated, he has softened intellectually and physically and become a harmonious component of a gentle, safe and childlike world in its simplicity. The Time Traveller's speculations are incorrect, but the voice is that of Wells, the social visionary, considering society's possible evolution and bursting out almost beyond the bounds of his narrative.

CHAPTER 5

Gazing from the hilltop as the moon rose in the heavens, the Traveller was stunned to discover that his Time Machine had vanished from the little lawn near the sphinxlike statue. Racing down the hill frantically, he thought of the possibility of never seeing his own age again. He fell once, cutting his face, but hurried on until he reached the spot where the machine had been. It was gone, indeed. Perhaps the gentle little people had sheltered it for him, but he could not escape the feeling that something unseen and unknown to him was responsible. Frantically, he ran and crawled about the nearby bushes, raving and shrieking, and even frightening off a white animal that he thought might have been a small deer. The Traveller then ran to the large hall where he had dined on fruit, lit matches, shouted and awoke the little people who were sleeping there. He cried out for his machine, but he was met by silly laughter from some and terror from others. Fear must have been forgotten by these creatures, he thought, and it was foolish to try to arouse it again. Leaving the great hall, he lay down near the white sphinx and fell asleep at last after much anguish and weeping.

In the morning he awoke clear-headed and calmer. Even if the Time Machine had been lost, he must be level-headed; perhaps he could discover the materials necessary to build another. Regardless, it was a beautiful and intriguing world in which he found himself. Probably the machine had only been hidden, and he would make every effort to recover it by cleverness or force. Unable to communicate with the laughing little people about his concern, the Traveller discovered some curious narrow footprints in the dirt near the sphinx. An examination of the bronze pedestal of the statue revealed that its sides contained panels much like doors. The conclusion was obvious; the machine was now inside the base of the huge statue. Further questioning of the little people produced nothing but a reaction of discomfort and loathing when the Traveller indicated that he wished the pedestal opened. Even a beating upon the panels with rocks produced nothing—except for what the Time Traveller interpreted as a faint chuckle from inside the pedestal—but then, he added, he must have been mistaken.

Thereafter, it appeared to him that the little people avoided him, but in a few days any apprehension they felt disappeared. He continued his efforts to learn their language, which seemed rather uncomplicated with no provision for abstractions or figurative expression—it was as uncomplicated as the minds of those who spoke it. In the days that followed, the Time Traveller never ventured very far from the location where he had arrived in the Time Machine. He viewed the splendid countryside from the tops of nearby hills, and his attention was soon drawn to the odd circular wells, covered with cupolas, that were situated here and there. Peering down one of these shafts, he could detect no bottom but could hear a distant dull thud like the sound of some great engine. He associated these wells with tall towers situated on the hillsides and speculated that the entire business was part of a vast underground ventilating system. This conclusion was to be proved completely false. These wells and towers were not the only puzzles facing the Time Traveller. In addition, he had noticed an absence of any sick or elderly among these little people, and no cemeteries or crematoria were evident. The people seemed to possess no machinery, devices or appliances of any kind, and seemed content simply to laugh and sing, make love playfully, eat fruit and decorate themselves with flowers. After three days among these gentle beings, the Time Traveller had learned very little about them and their world of the year 802,701 A.D.

At last the Time Traveller made a fast friend, a tiny little woman whose name he learned was Weena. He had rescued her from the main current of a stream where she was being swept away, for the basic weakness of these creatures made them helpless even in water that moved at moderate speed. Thereafter, Weena clung with childish affection to the Time Traveller, following him closely and obviously devoted to him in every possible way. It was a strange friendship, and it was to endure only a week. From Weena the Traveller learned that fear was not extinct among these people, for this tiny woman cringed from dark and shadowy places, a fact which made the Traveller recollect that these people slept together at night in large groups within the great halls. Regardless, the Traveller slept apart from these huddled crowds, to the temporary dismay of Weena. Her affection for him, however, replaced most of her apprehension. On the night before he had rescued Weena from the water, the Time Traveller awoke suddenly with the impression that some grayish creature had just fled from the spot where he slept. Unable to sleep, he decided to watch the dawn. Gazing at the cheerless sky, he fancied he saw white apelike creatures running up a distant hill, carrying what appeared to be a body. It was very early, of course, and he was uncertain at the time if he saw this at all. Daylight came and there were no scurrying white figures. Ghosts, mused the Time Traveller, but still he could not help associating these figures with the curious white animal he had surprised in his frantic search through the bushes for his Time Machine. Soon enough the deadly reality of this ghostly morning vision would be all too clear to him.

On the morning of the fourth day it was very hot, and as usual, hotter than it was in the Time Traveller's age. Seeking some shelter from the oppressive heat in a ruin near the great building where he slept, the Traveller came upon a dark shadowy area obscured from the sunlight. Suddenly, he encountered a pair of shining eyes observing him from the darkness. Recalling the little people's terror of darkness, the Traveller moved toward the shape before him and spoke to it somewhat shakily. It flashed past him and headed down into the sunlight, white and apelike with reddish eyes, stumbling and groping into a tumble of dark ruins a short distance away. When he pursued the creature, it seemed to the Time Traveller that it had disappeared into a well that was half-concealed by some fallen stonework. Peering down the opening, he noticed a series of rungs leading downward—and also a pair of reddish eyes disappearing into the blackness below.

Surely, speculated the Time Traveller, man had evolved into two distinct species, the graceful happy creatures on the earth's surface, and these apelike night creatures living below ground. This Golden Age was not as golden as it seemed at first, and he began to consider once more the bronze doors of the sphinx and to suspect what might have happened to his machine. However, he imagined that he could see the way in which this division of species occurred. It was social and economic. It was the ancient division between capitalist and laborer that had brought about the tunneling of this strange species underground. An effort has always been made to get the less decorous industrial and economic functions of society into underground spaces. In the course of the ages then, industry and its laborers had lost their claim to the upper world and had slipped permanently beneath the ground. The continual refinement process of the rich and their intense higher educational process ever widened the gap between classes. The system continued with the rich pursuing beauty, pleasure and leisure on the surface of the earth, while the worker became more and more adapted to his underground life until it became part of his very nature. Simply put, it was a question of the Haves and Have-nots. Consequently, concluded the Time Traveller, man had not executed a great triumph simply over Nature, but over other men as well. A point of ideal balance in society had been reached in some past age, and this was the result; a dwindled, decadent humanity. These laughing, playful Upper-worlders, or Eloi as they were called, were man diminished in size and brain power. Those Under-grounders (called Morlocks, the Time Traveller would discover shortly) were an even greater departure from the human type.

The Traveller concluded that the Morlocks had taken the Time Machine, but wondered why the Eloi of the Upper-world, if they were the masters, had not returned it to him. The Eloi's fear of darkness also occupied his thoughts. When he questioned Weena about these things, she was brought to tears, and the Time Traveller hastened to restore her laughter and smiles with the sparkle and flicker of a lighted match.

COMMENT: With the introduction of the Morlocks, or underground people, this Golden Age of the future has become less ideal. Here, once again, Wells is the speculative social philosopher interpreting surface and subterranean worlds and their mutated inhabitants as the degenerative result of class division: capital and labor, upper and lower class, the Haves and the Have-nots. The Time Traveller, Wells's persona or literary mask, observes that even in the London of his day, workers "live in such artificial conditions as practically to be cut off from the natural surface of the earth."

The marks of the author's reforming zeal are visible in *The Time Machine,* his first great scientific romance; and gradually they would become the dominant characteristics of his later books. Wells was never to forsake the elements of fictionalized science in his work, but by the time we encounter *Tono-Bungay,* the full-bodied social reformer is squarely before us.

It should be noted also that if the Time Traveller is Wells's persona, or literary personality, he represents a thoroughly transparent one. In his periodic social speculations and commentary, the Traveller more and more can be seen to be Wells himself. Little success is evident in creating a literary character distinct from its author. Wells speaks; Wells travels to the future. Wells is the central figure, and we shall encounter this more than once in the other novels to be examined in this guide.

CHAPTER 6

The Time Traveller soon acquired the same revulsion for the Morlocks that the Eloi had. As the moon was soon to pass through its final quarter, the Traveller realized that the nights would become darker and possibly the Morlocks would be more in evidence. Uneasy and insecure, he increased the range of his explorations about the countryside, observing in the distance a great bluish-green building, oriental in appearance, and surely having once served some special purpose. However, the Time Traveller did not permit this Palace of Green Porcelain, as he called it, to become an excuse for delaying what he knew he must do—descend one of the well shafts to explore whatever waited in the Under-world of the Morlocks.

One of the shafts was chosen and he began to descend by means of metallic rungs on its walls. Reluctantly the Traveller left Weena distraught and pleading above. For some two hundred yards he proceeded down, once nearly falling, and finally pained and exhausted he rested in a narrow tunnel which opened upon the shaft. After resting for some time, he was startled by the soft cold touch of three Morlocks who quickly fled as he lit a match into sputtering brilliance before them. From the darkness their reddish eyes glittered as they watched him, and the Traveller soon discovered that their language was different from that of the Eloi—communication was impossible. He crawled along the narrow tunnel as the noise of what seemed to be heavy machinery grew louder. Suddenly he came upon a large cavern, where in the pale flickering of his match the Time Traveller could make out bulky shapes like great machines, and the cowering outlines of Morlocks withdrawn from the light. There was a table upon which part of a large slaughtered animal rested. It was a meal, no doubt. The Morlocks were carnivorous. The scent of fresh blood hung in the air, and the Time Traveller tried to imagine what large red-blooded animal had survived into this age to provide the Morlocks' meal.

He had squandered most of his matches in amusing the Eloi and now discovered that only four remained. How ill-equipped I am, he thought, for this undertaking. He had expected a world of remarkable scientific advancement and perfection, and there he was with matches as weapons against these vile little apelike creatures that even now began to swarm over him, unafraid of him in the dark. Breaking free, he was pursued down the tunnel to the shaft. The

Traveller grasped the rungs and kicked free of the Morlocks. He climbed up toward the world of light, leaving behind those revolting creatures with their blinking red eyes and chinless inhuman faces. Once at the surface, exhausted and semiconscious, he was aware of Weena clinging to him and kissing him excitedly.

COMMENT: The Time Traveller has experienced the horror of the Morlocks' world. He now sees the incredible division between the Eloi, a people of laughter, childish happiness, and light—and the foul-smelling whitish creatures who thrive in darkness in the bowels of the earth. The year 802,701 A.D. is no utopian paradise after all.

CHAPTER 7

Assuredly, the Morlocks threatened the Time Traveller's hope of recovering his lost machine. The harmless and playful little Eloi had never been a real impediment to its recovery, but these Morlocks seemed inhuman and evil, and the Time Traveller loathed them. The new moon with its attendant darkness was near at hand, and he felt that the Morlocks waited only for the proper time to rush upon him. He now believed that his theory of the class divisions intensified by capital and labor was not the source of the grim condition of the world he now faced. Perhaps the Eloi were once privileged aristocracy and the Morlocks their servants. The Eloi may have degenerated to their present state of "beautiful futility." Now it might be that the positions were reversing, the Eloi allowed to inhabit the surface, while the Morlocks, once the subjects, were now the masters, clothing the Eloi and maintaining them almost as cattle. Why? And then the sight of the freshly slaughtered meat he had seen in the Morlocks' cavern entered the Time Traveller's thoughts once again. Yes, he mused, man had cast his brother out of light and comfort and now the scales were balancing.

His mind turned from further speculation to a need of defense against the present danger, and he realized the need for weapons and a place to fortify against the Morlocks. Exploring along the Thames valley he discovered nothing suitable, but suddenly he remembered the Palace of Green Porcelain he had thought of visiting before the descent into the Morlocks' well. With Weena on his shoulders the Time Traveller set out toward the Palace, which he discovered to be some eighteen miles off, more than twice the distance he had reckoned at first. After a while Weena ran beside him, placing flowers in his pockets, for the pockets on his clothes had from the beginning seemed mysterious to her.

Pausing in his tale, the Time Traveller withdrew two large white withered flowers from his pocket, placed them on the table before his attentive guests, and proceeded with his tale.

He and Weena had walked toward what was once Wimbledon. Weena grew tired, the shadows lengthened, and the Time Traveller feared entering the dense woods that now lay before them. He could not see the Porcelain Palace and so decided to spend the night on the open hillside. He dozed from time to time and, gazing up at the heavens, became aware that all the familiar constellations had disappeared from the heavens and new arrangements among the stars had replaced them. How many civilizations, languages, literatures, had come and gone with only the pitiful Eloi and their foul brothers beneath the earth as the sole inheritors of man's high aspirations? He thought of the fear that the Eloi felt for the Morlocks and suddenly was struck by suspicions of what that fresh meat in the Morlocks' subterranean chamber might really be—but it was too grotesque, and the sight of tiny Weena sleeping beside him helped to dismiss the thought.

In the morning, he realized that his ankle was swollen. One of his shoes had recently lost a heel and his foot had now become painful. He removed his shoes and discarded them. As the day grew brighter, Weena awoke and they found fruit to eat. They met some of the Eloi dancing and laughing gaily as though the dreaded night and the Morlocks did not exist. At some time, thought the Time Traveller, the Morlocks' food supplies had diminished and at last they had turned—elsewhere. Even in our own time, thought the Time Traveller, man has become less selective in his food than he once was—and furthermore, man's nature does not irrevocably oppose him to the eating of human flesh. The Time Traveller attempted to rationalize the realization he had finally come to accept. He tried to be objective. After all, he reasoned, these Eloi were nothing more than cattle, probably preserved and bred by the Morlocks. Besides, it was humanity's just reward for its timeless selfishness—the Eloi brain was feeble; and in the final decadence of aristocracy, man had become little more than meat for those upon whose labors he had once thrived. But the Traveller could not maintain this philosophical detachment, for the presence of Weena beside him and the still human appearance of the Eloi bound him sympathetically to them—

and made him share their fear as well. He had, however, several ideas about what should be done to protect himself against the Morlocks. He would require a safe refuge, some stone or metal weapons — and the ingredients for a torch, which would certainly be his most formidable weapon against these Under-world creatures. Something would be needed to batter down the bronze doors of the sphinx where he was certain the Time Machine would be found. He could then return to his own age bringing Weena with him. With these things in mind, he pressed on toward the Palace of Green Porcelain.

COMMENT: At first, this world of the future had seemed to be a green paradise populated by a happy dancing people, delicate and intellectually feeble. Gradually, the apparent utopia has revealed itself to be a nightmare. There is the world above preyed upon by the Morlock world below. The reason for the Eloi fear of the dark has now dawned upon the Time Traveller in all its horror; the Eloi are kept and slaughtered as meat for the Morlocks. The Time Traveller himself is now an enemy of these night creatures and is swept by the same fear experienced by the Eloi.

It is interesting to observe how Wells gradually provides the reasons for the Time Traveller's ragged and bruised condition when he suddenly appeared before his dinner guests. In this chapter his feet have become sore and swollen, and he has discarded his shoes; it will be recalled that part of his singular appearance upon his return was the fact that he wore only a pair of bloody socks on his feet.

Wells is careful also to include contemporary place names in his descriptions of the countryside. This is not some distant planet he has traveled to, but England itself. He has moved through time, but not through space.

CHAPTER 8

When he arrived at the Palace of Green Porcelain, the Time Traveller entered and discovered that it had once been a great museum. He discovered fossils and the skeletons of huge prehistoric beasts. Much of what he discovered was remarkably preserved because bacteria and fungi had disappeared from the world in this incredible future age. However, decay could not be halted altogether, and gradually it had made its inroads on the exhibits. It was silent in the museum as the Traveller gazed about and Weena played with a sea urchin on one of the glass cases. From the paleontological exhibits, he and Weena moved on to an area devoted to natural history and one containing a display of huge machines, many broken and badly corroded. The Time Traveller confessed that he had a great weakness for mechanisms but could only guess at the original purpose of these. As they wandered along this particular gallery, it was Weena who noticed that the end of the large room was veiled in darkness. The room, seemingly built into a hill, came up against the ground outside and had only narrow slits of windows to admit light. The Time Traveller became aware that the heavy dust which covered the floor elsewhere was less abundant here. He spied sets of narrow footprints and was immediately conscious of the same strange noises he had heard down the Morlocks' well. There was no doubt that the Morlocks were there, and so the Time Traveller seized a protruding lever from one of the huge machines nearby, wrenched it off and at last had himself a most formidable weapon. Overcoming a strong desire to venture into the shadows and kill some of the Morlocks, the Traveller took Weena and proceeded into another section of the ruined museum where he encountered the covers and clasps of old books; the contents had long since turned to dust. He contemplated the great futility of human effort to which this heap of remains bore witness. He thought, too, of his own published papers on physical optics.

In a room devoted to physical chemistry, the Time Traveller came upon a great discovery—a box of matches, perfectly preserved. He cried out with joy and called for Weena to join him as he danced about ecstatically. In addition, he discovered some camphor which he recalled was inflammable and would serve them handsomely as a candle. He chanced upon some old rifles and pistols, some of which, made of some strange metal, had avoided much of the rust that had infected the other weapons. He discovered a hatchet and a sword also, but decided on the crowbarlike lever he had wrenched from one of the great machines. Then, disappointed at finding two dynamite sticks to be dummies, the Time Traveller and Weena wandered on through the museum until they came to a small open court. They ate fruit from several trees that grew there. The Time Traveller now had weapons to use against the Morlocks; as daylight would soon be gone, he decided that it would be wisest to pass the night in the open once again. His courage and his spirits had been raised by his fortunate discoveries in the museum, and on the following day there would be the business of the bronze doors of the white sphinx and the recovery of his Time Machine.

CHAPTER 9

When they had left the museum, there was still some daylight remaining. The Time Traveller intended to reach the sphinx the next morning and hoped before darkness to cross through the forbidding woods that had halted them previously. They would proceed as far as possible and then light a fire of dried sticks and foliage gathered along the way. The Time Traveller had not slept for two days and drowsiness was beginning to creep over him. In some dark shrubbery he spied three crouching figures but hastened on as the woods seemed to be only a mile across. His camphor and matches would protect them, but the firewood and dried brush had become awkward to carry. It struck the Time Traveller suddenly that he would light a fire with them right there as a deterrent to the Morlocks he knew were close behind. It was, in fact, a deadly mistake. Weena was fascinated and would have leaped into the blaze had not the Time Traveller picked her up bodily and plunged on into the forest ahead. In no time at all he could hear the patter of the Morlocks' footsteps behind them. Suddenly they were all about him clawing and pulling at his clothes. Weena slid to the ground as the Time Traveller drove the Morlocks off with a lighted match. He then lit a camphor ball, and its sputtering brilliance kept the murmuring Morlocks at their distance. Weena had fainted; and as the Time Traveller raised her in his arms, he was stunned by an awareness that in the scuffle with the Morlocks he had lost his sense of direction completely. Unable to get his bearings he decided to build a fire and make camp on the spot. The camphor sputtered out. As he struck a match, he blinded a Morlock who was rushing towards Weena and smashed the creature to the ground with his fist. The foliage was quite dry, for there had been no rain during the week since his arrival in the Time Machine. The Time Traveller gathered dried brush, sticks and green wood and lit a fire that poured off a thick billowing smoke.

Secure in the impression that the fire would be good for an hour, the Time Traveller must have dozed from the heaviness of the smoke and camphor fumes. Suddenly he was overwhelmed by Morlocks. The fire had gone out and the unholy creatures were upon him. They tore at him, bit his neck, and he was only able to free himself after a series of vicious blows with the iron lever he had acquired in the Palace of Green Porcelain. As the Morlock attack slackened, the Time Traveller realized that he alone was not responsible for their sudden change of mind. The forest was ablaze; and the Morlocks, terrified by the fire and light, rushed about in a frenzy. The fire roared on, the very fire the Time Traveller had started himself as a deterrent to the pursuing Morlocks. Weena had disappeared and was nowhere to be seen. Morlocks ran madly in all directions, and the Time Traveller struck at many that rushed toward him before realizing that they had become blinded and helpless from the light. Driven to the brink of anguish and despair, the Time Traveller beat the ground with his fists and cried out to God to end this hideous nightmare. Through the remainder of the night, he struck down any Morlocks that careened into him in their howling terror and blindness. He did his best to avoid the consuming flames that lit the sky by remaining on a small rise of land that sat like an island in the middle of the forest.

With the brightness of day he became wretched at the thought of dear little Weena's death. Surely the Morlocks had left her body in the woods, but that at least was a better end than what they had intended for her. When some of the smoke had cleared, the Time Traveller regained his sense of direction, tied some grass to his feet, and with a limp made his way over the hot earth toward the white sphinx — and the Time Machine. He was exhausted and touched with a terrible sense of loneliness but was cheered to a degree by the discovery of some matches in his pocket that had survived the ferocious struggle with the Morlocks.

CHAPTER 10

By eight or nine o'clock in the morning the Time Traveller had arrived at the little hill and the twisted seat of yellowish metal from which he had surveyed this future world upon his arrival a week ago. He thought of the Eloi, gentle and beautiful and no more than cattle. How brief had been humanity's triumph. A perfect world of comfort, security and ease had been attained, no doubt; but it was suicidal for mankind. Without need, without danger, without challenge, there had been no demand upon intelligence. Perfect harmony had bred only feebleness. The Under-world laborers involved with their machines perhaps retained a degree of drive and intellectual activity, although becoming less human in appearance than the Upperworld people. It may have been that faced with a loss of whatever meat supply they had, these underground creatures took to eating the Upper-worlders. His meditations led to drowsiness, and soon the Time Traveller yielded to the luxury of a long and refreshing sleep.

When he awoke near sunset, he felt secure from any sleepiness in the face of the Morlocks. When he approached the sphinx he was startled to discover that the bronze panels on the statue had been lowered and that he was free to enter. There, within the statue and elevated somewhat, was the Time Machine, which obviously had been disassembled and then put together again by the Morlocks in a futile effort to comprehend its purpose. The Time Traveller understood at once that the Morlocks meant to trap him. Somewhat amused, he entered the sphinx clutching his matches and the forward and reverse levers for the machine. At once it struck him that the matches required a box for striking, but in a moment the bronze panels had shut behind him. As he hastened to put the levers in place, the Morlocks surged forward and swarmed over him, nearly wrenching one of the levers from his hand. It was a close struggle, worse than the one in the forest; but when the levers were in place and the machine activated, the clawing Morlocks fell away and the Time Traveller passed into that dull light and violent motion he had experienced at the beginning of his journey.

CHAPTER 11

In his haste to escape from the Morlocks and the year 802,701 A.D., the Time Traveller had inadvertently thrust the levers into the forward position. Rather than moving back through time toward his own age, he was racing wildly into the future. Traveling at tremendous speed, the change from night to day soon became less rapid until he realized that the sun no longer set but simply rose and fell in the western sky. It seemed to have become broader and redder in appearance. At last, the sun hung motionless on the horizon, occasionally brightening or experiencing a momentary extinction. The earth had finally come to rest with one side toward the dull red of the sun, and the great tidal movements had ceased to be. Slowly the Traveller reversed the levers of the Time Machine until his furious pace began to slow and the vague proportions of a deserted beach stretched out before him. Above, the sky was a deep red and brightened in the distance where the sun's scarlet mass had been slashed by the horizon. Great reddish rocks lay about touched with green vegetation on their sunward sides. As the Traveller observed that there was no wind and that no waves broke upon the desolate shore, he was startled by the fact that one of the great reddish rocks he had noticed now moved toward him. It was actually a great crab, eyes protruding on stalks, antennae waving and with a shell corrugated and encrusted with green slime. Something touched him from behind, and he whirled to see another of these hideous creatures, grotesque with slime and about to destroy him. The Traveller's hand was quickly upon the levers, and he sped forward in time, at first a hundred years and then at leaps of a thousand or more. The sun was growing larger, and life upon the ancient earth gradually died away.

He was now thirty million years into the future. It was difficult to breathe and had become cold, with fringes of ice along the edge of the sea and snow visible on the higher inland slopes. Once the Time Traveller imagined he saw some black object moving about on the shoals but decided that he was deceived in the uncertain light. The heavens began to grow dark and the air was chilled as a massive eclipse of the sun by some planet took place. The Traveller became nauseous and his labored breathing had weakened him. Sick and confused, he realized that there was some sort of round black creature with tentacles moving about on the distant shoal. Terrified at the thought of losing consciousness on that forsaken beach of the future, the Time Traveller pulled himself into the saddle of the machine and hurtled the mechanism toward his own age.

COMMENT: The Traveller has journeyed to the far reaches of the future, to that fearsome time when humanity has long since vanished and all life as we know it has become extinct. Still, there is that odd black shape scurrying about on the shoal as the grand, yet terrifying, eclipse of the dying sun seems to suggest the final labored movements of the universe. That black tentacled creature—what was it?—perhaps some grim mutation of human or animal life, but a species that the Time Traveller will not take the opportunity to investigate, here where he is merely a vulnerable anachronism, a flesh and blood antiquity incredibly present at the last groans of creation.

CHAPTER 12

Thus, the Time Traveller returned to his own age. At first he sped backwards in time at the usual incredible rate, but gradually the walls of his laboratory took shape around him. As the machine slowed, the Traveller saw his housekeeper move backward through one door in the room, slowly cross it and move out another door, the very reverse of what he had seen her do as he began his trip through time. Then she had seemed to flash across the room at dazzling speed. He had now moved backward in time; and, therefore, the movement of things reversed themselves before his eyes as the Time Machine slowed and was brought to a halt. The only difference was that the machine now rested in an opposite corner of the laboratory, this being the distance that the Morlocks had moved it from the grassy plot on which it had rested to its hiding place within the base of the white sphinx. Once again in his laboratory, the Time Traveller had climbed down and made his way dizzily to the dining room where his guests awaited him.

The story was now told and the Time Traveller paused to observe the effect of his tale upon his friends. There was a shuffling of feet, and the editor remarked that it was a shame that their host did not write stories. The tale had been met with disbelief, and the Traveller said he did not blame them for skepticism, so incredible did the adventure seem even to him. Upon the table before him lay the withered white flowers. This was puzzling to the medical man, for upon examination he could not identify them. The Time Traveller would not give them up and, with apparent confusion and uncertainty about his own thoughts, declared that they had been put in his pocket by his little Eloi friend Weena. Suddenly, he seized a lamp and made his way to the laboratory, the narrator following him. There was the Time Machine before them, stained and splattered, with some turf clinging to the lower parts of it, and with one of its rails bent out of shape. The Time Traveller sighed with relief. The story *was* true, and the doubts that had suddenly thrust themselves upon him were now gone. He *had* traveled through time.

The guests now left, and the medical man hastened to observe that their host was suffering from overwork, an observation which drew a hearty laugh from the Time Traveller.

Perplexed and sleepless from most of that night, the narrator returned on the following day to the Time Traveller's laboratory to find him busily preparing for another journey. This time there would be proof, he said, a camera would be used and a specimen brought back besides. A half-hour would be all he needed; and if the narrator would just sit and read some magazines, he would be back with solid proof of his time traveling. The narrator was seated only a few moments when he recalled an important appointment and hastened down the corridor to the laboratory to tell the Time Traveller that he could not wait. As he entered the lab, he was met by some odd noise and a rush of air that swirled about him. The Time Traveller was not there, and the narrator was faced with a swirling transparent shape with a hazy figure seated in the midst of it. Suddenly it vanished, and the narrator stared in disbelief. At that moment, a servant entered the lab from a door at the other end and confirmed the fact that the Time Traveller had not left by way of the garden at the rear. The narrator waited awhile, but the Traveller did not return. That was three years ago, and in fact he has never returned.

EPILOGUE

One must ever wonder, mused the narrator, if the Time Traveller will ever return. Perhaps he journeyed into man's past this time and fell among savages and the terrors of great prehistoric creatures. Yet, he may have traveled into a future time when men were still recognizable as such, into the maturity of the race when many of the clumsy gropings of our own day would be answered and satisfied. Certainly, the ineffectual experimenting and theorizing of today does not represent man's peak of achievement. Perhaps the progress of mankind is but the building of a towering heap that must in the end tumble upon those who built it. If this is the case, man must live as though it were not true. For him, observed the narrator, the future remains darkly impenetrable, yielding only momentarily to the fragmentary light offered by the Time Traveller's story. All that remained now for the narrator were the two faded and shriveled white flowers, a reminder that when all else had failed man, there yet remained to him the touch of gratitude and a tender affection.

COMMENT: In this Epilogue, Wells speaks out with a mixture of hope, despair and stoicism. There must be hope for a time when man will be better than he is. It cannot be man's fulfillment merely to blunder along in error and feeble theory. Man must look to the future and see himself still in the process of "becoming." However, Wells suggests, it may well be that man's progress is a progression only to ruin and self-destruction. Failure may reward humanity's struggle. Nonetheless, man must maintain himself as though whatever grim future lay before him was, indeed, not there at all.

Up to this point Wells had divided his persona, or literary personality, between the Time Traveller and the narrator. Now, as the Traveller remains somewhere in time like a visionary pilgrim wandering the paths of man's decline or restoration, Wells speaks out strongly in the voice of the narrator, left behind to reflect somberly on the state of the human condition, consoled in part by an awareness that in man's last infirmity, the capacity for warmth and gentle communion remained compassionately in the human spirit.

THE INVISIBLE MAN

CHAPTER 1
The Strange Man's Arrival

He had arrived one cold and snowy February day at the Coach and
Horses Inn in Iping and had called out immediately for a room and a
fire to warm himself. After agreeing to terms, Mrs. Hall, the landlady, had left him in his quarters and had gone to prepare a meal,
congratulating herself as she did on the good fortune to have a paying guest in winter. On her return with plates and table linens, she
was surprised to see that despite the warm fire in the room her guest
still had his hat and coat on as he stood staring out the window. To
her suggestion that she take them, he replied that he preferred to
keep them on. She noticed that he wore heavy dark glasses with
blinders on the sides and that he had heavy side whiskers, the result
being that with his hat and coat on, his face was completely hidden.
When she returned once again with his lunch, he did not turn about
from his place at the window until she was closing the door on her
way out. But then she remembered the mustard. She had forgotten it
and hurried to berate Millie, the kitchen help, who had dawdled in
its preparation. As she returned to the stranger's room with the mustard, she burst in after a hasty knock. He bent down quickly as if to
pick up something from the floor. When she had gathered up the wet
clothes and boots, Mrs. Hall turned to face her guest and was startled to find him covering the lower part of his face with a napkin.
Leave the hat, he said, his head swathed in bandages with wisps of
thick black hair protruding between the windings. He wore a jacket
with the collar turned up, and so all that was really visible of him
was the shiny pinkness of his nose. He wore brown gloves, and his
large blue glasses remained in place. Mrs. Hall regained her composure somewhat and awkwardly made her way from the room with
the promise that she would have the clothes dried promptly. The
poor man has had an accident or an operation, mused Mrs. Hall as
she hung up the stranger's clothes.

When she came to clear away the lunch dishes, her guest sat smoking a pipe with a white scarf wrapped about the lower part of his

face. He announced that he had some luggage at Bramblehurat station and was rather disappointed to learn that it could not be brought to the inn until the following day. It was a dangerous road, and people had been killed on it, he was told. Accidents happen you know, she added, in an effort to engage the man in conversation. Her own nephew had had an accident, and there was the fear of an operation and. . . . The stranger abruptly asked for matches, and Mrs. Hall's oration was cut short. His curt manner had irritated her, and she was rather short and disagreeable with poor Millie for the remainder of the afternoon. As for the stranger, he remained smoking by the fire and might have been heard pacing from time to time and mumbling to himself.

CHAPTER 2
Mr. Teddy Henfrey's First Impressions

Mr. Teddy Henfrey's business was clocks. He had come out of the falling snow and into the bar at about four o'clock when Mrs. Hall was trying to be courageous enough to inquire if her strange new guest wished tea. The clock in the parlor required some repair; and then with Mr. Henfrey in tow, she rapped upon the door and entered abruptly upon her guest dozing in an armchair. His bandaged head had drooped to one side, and it appeared to her in the half light that his mouth was enormous, engulfing the entire lower portion of his face. The light had played tricks, she thought, and as the stranger sat up startled, he quickly held his muffler to his face. Teddy Henfrey was admitted with politeness, and the stranger inquired of Mrs. Hall if his baggage could not possibly be brought over before tomorrow. It could not, she responded coldly, and the stranger hastened to explain that he was an "experimental investigator." Mrs. Hall was impressed. He required solitude and freedom from intrusion. He had sustained an accident, and this confirmed Mrs. Hall's earlier conjectures. Mrs. Hall was most understanding and was about to respond when the stranger cut her off once again, and she left the room. The stranger now stood by the fire and concentrated his attention upon Teddy Henfrey, who had made his repair of the clock intentionally slow and was all too obvious about it. As Henfrey stalled and fumbled at his work, he looked up to see the stranger's gaze fixed firmly upon him. Be done with it and go, barked the stranger. Mr. Henfrey stammered a bit, made a quick adjustment on the clock and was gone.

At Gleeson's corner Teddy Henfrey met Mr. Hall, whose horse-drawn cart was the town conveyance and who evidently had stopped at several pubs on the way from Sidderbridge Junction. Teddy Henfrey then proceeded to describe the odd stranger at the inn and his equally odd behavior. Hall himself would see to it and drove off to see just what manner of person his wife had given quarters to. At about half past nine, when the stranger had retired and Hall had received sharp words from his wife about his delayed return, he strode masterfully into the parlor, looked about authoritatively, and examined a sheet of computations the stranger had left behind.

That night Mrs. Hall dreamed of huge heads wrapped up in white and looking like great turnips. But she was a sensible sort, and so upon awakening, simply dispelled her fears and went back to sleep.

CHAPTER 3
The Thousand and One Bottles

On the twenty-ninth of February, the day after his arrival, the stranger's luggage was brought up through the slush and snow. There were crates, boxes, cases, cartons of fat books, and a couple of trunks. The whole business was brought up in Fearenside's cart. Hall had been gossiping with Fearenside, and the stranger all wrapped up came impatiently out to hurry them up. He did not see Fearenside's dog, who growled fiercely, and proceeded to lunge at his gloved hand, finally biting his leg and tearing the stranger's trousers in the bargain. As the cartman routed the dog, the stranger hastened into the inn and the seclusion of his quarters. Hall ran after him and followed right into the man's room. In the dim light, a handless arm was thrust at him, and he was struck violently upon the chest and thrust back through the door which was then slammed in his face. Out in the street once more, Hall was too bewildered by what had occurred and too inarticulate to express it adequately and so simply decided that the fellow upstairs didn't want any help at the moment. In a few moments, the mysterious guest appeared once more, this time wearing different trousers and gloves and announcing that the dog bite had not even broken the skin. However, he was most anxious to get on with unloading the baggage.

When the first crate was brought into the parlor, the stranger set upon it avidly, emptying it of the various shaped bottles it contained and scattering the straw about the floor. He maintained this pace until six cases had been emptied of a great abundance of bottles. He then set to work at once and did not hear Mrs. Hall when she brought him his dinner. He looked up for a moment, then quickly turned away, and it struck her for an instant that his eye sockets were exceptionally hollow. He put on his spectacles and forestalled her objection to the scattered straw by requesting that no one enter without knocking, so intense and so urgent was the nature of his investigations. A reference to the straw on her part was met by his suggestion that she add the cost of any inconvenience to his bill—a shilling would do nicely. When he worked that afternoon, the door remained locked; and there emerged the sounds of erratic pacing, violent thumping and the rattle of bottles. Once Mrs. Hall could hear her guest raving about his inability to go on and cries of "cheated" and "fool" and "liar." Mrs. Hall brought in tea, and when she noticed broken glass and stains upon her carpet, she was told simply to add it to the bill.

At the Iping Hanger tavern that afternoon, Fearenside remarked to Teddy Henfrey that the strange guest at the inn must be black since there was only blackness where his dog had bitten the fellow, nothing that even looked like skin. He's a "piebald," observed Fearenside, a half-breed with light and dark patches all over him, the way it is with horses. Certainly an odd thing, said Teddy, and him with his pink nose too.

COMMENT: The mystery surrounding the bizarre visitor at Iping continues to deepen. However, Wells hints that his strangeness is more than eccentricity, and we are allowed but momentary glimpses of the nothingness that lies behind his wrappings. He is fierce, terrifying in manner; and his raving suggests madness. It is interesting to note that Wells pairs off the frightening aspect of the stranger with the humorous and rustic ignorance of the townsfolk. We are given, therefore, some assurance of the direction that Wells's narrative will assume—one of mystery and terror, but one that is brushed with the comic also.

CHAPTER 4
Mr. Cuss Interviews the Stranger

Until late April and the first indications of money problems, the stranger had always handled his little encounters with Mrs. Hall by the addition of a small sum to his bill. Mr. Hall had never liked the fellow and often alluded to the possibility of ridding themselves of him. Mrs. Hall was none too fond of him either but was practical enough to admit that there was something to be said for bills paid promptly. The stranger did not attend church, one day being the same as another in his fitful commitment to work. He talked to himself, occasionally smashed things, and seemed a man ridden and possessed by some obsession. He rarely ventured out during the day; but at twilight he would take to the loneliest paths, occasionally to encounter and startle some person homeward bound.

Mrs. Hall felt quite superior whenever she announced that her guest was an experimental investigator. He discovered things, she said, and had suffered an accident discoloring his face and hands and was most sensitive to any public attention. Some townsfolk, mainly Mr. Teddy Henfrey, reckoned that he might be a criminal at large, but there was no significant crime of long standing to which he might be conveniently assigned. To some he was an anarchist, to others a simple lunatic, and a suspicion of the supernatural was not altogether dismissed by others. Everyone, though, was in agreement in disliking him, and even the children chimed in by calling "Bogey man" after him and then scurrying off elatedly.

The stranger had stirred the curiosity of Mr. Cuss, the town doctor, who, under the ruse of a subscription list for a village nurse, decided to get a closer look at this curious guest residing at the inn. Mrs. Hall did not know his name; but even without the advantage of this information, Cuss tapped upon the parlor door and entered to the litany of growling threats. Mrs. Hall could hear voices for some ten minutes or so when suddenly she heard an exclamation of surprise from within, a chair overturn, some hasty footsteps, and then saw Mr. Cuss appear, his face ashen and peering back over his shoulder. The stranger could be heard laughing and immediately the parlor door was slammed shut.

Cuss hastened to the lodgings of Bunting, the vicar, and his agitation had to be satisfied with some of that good minister's cheap sherry.

He had gotten in to see the fellow, he related, with the stranger most disagreeable and cross at the intrusion. Yes, the man was researching. He had lost a valuable medical prescription, blown into the fire and gone up in smoke. Swish—and the stranger had gestured with his arm. But, added the animated Cuss, there was no hand, just an empty sleeve. The fellow had a stout cough and cold for himself and sniffed all the while. But that sleeve, added Cuss, empty—and yet how could you move an empty sleeve? It was empty all right, and he brought it right up to my face and something like fingers and a thumb actually tweaked my nose. The vicar laughed but Cuss's fright was honest enough. He had struck at the sleeve and it felt just like hitting an arm. Bunting considered the report he had just heard and remarked quite profoundly that it was indeed a most remarkable account.

COMMENT: As the facts about the mysterious stranger become more puzzling, we realize, too, that he had retained a sense of bizarre humor, precious little comfort, though, from the torment and wretchedness he is enduring. He appears to have no arm and no hand, but there is something solid in that sleeve. Mrs. Hall had thought his eye sockets extremely hollow when she caught a fleeting glimpse of them in a dim light. In addition, his mouth looked enormous and there seemed to be nothing in his trouser leg when he was bitten by the dog. Parts of his body, therefore, are invisible; and in his experiments he is tormented by a failure to discover a prescription that he lost by accident. What is this man's secret? What is the source of his agony?—and what is the cause of his invisibility?

CHAPTER 5
The Burglary at the Vicarage

In the still hours before dawn on Whit Monday, the vicarage had been burglarized; and the related facts were broadcast by the vicar and his wife themselves. His wife had roused the Rev. Mr. Bunting, who had descended to his study to investigate a noise. Hearing a sneeze from the direction of the study, he armed himself with a stout poker and pressed on. At the half-opened door, the vicar could hear movement from within, a drawer opened, papers rustled; there was an oath and he could see a lighted candle upon the desk—but no intruder was visible. At the sound of jingling coins, the vicar rushed into the room with Mrs. Bunting close behind; but to their amazement, it was empty. They stared—dumbfounded. Nothing under the desk. Nothing behind the screen. But then a sneeze in the hall. The couple tumbled out of the study in time to see the scullery door open at the other end of the kitchen and then slam violently shut a moment later—but still no intruder could be seen. It was marvelous indeed, and by daylight the vicar and his wife were still awake and thoroughly perplexed.

COMMENT: It should be noted here that the vicar and his wife heard violent sneezing. In the previous chapter, Mr. Cuss, the medical man, had observed that the mysterious stranger had obviously caught a heavy cold, and so it becomes rather obvious that the invisible man has been prowling about the vicarage. Coins were heard to jingle, and it may be that the stranger's funds had now run short, obliging him to replenish them however and wherever he could.

CHAPTER 6
The Furniture That Went Mad

Very early on Whit Monday morning, Mr. and Mrs. Hall were in the basement of the inn seeing to the good health of their beer. Mr. Hall had come upstairs for some forgotten sarsaparilla and observed that the stranger's door was ajar and that the front door was not bolted as he knew it had been the night before. He peered into the stranger's room and discovered it to be empty, save for the fact that the only clothes the guest was known to possess were scattered about. Mrs. Hall was soon up from the cellar bristling with impatience. Later, they agreed on having thought they heard the front door open and close, but no one seemed to enter or leave to confirm the suspicion. Mrs. Hall went on ahead of her husband toward the stranger's room as a sneeze was heard on the stairway. Each believed it had come from the other, as apparently there was no one else in the building. Once in the room, incredible things occurred. Bedclothes, the stranger's hat, a chair and other objects went flying through the air. There was a hoarse laugh, and the Halls were suddenly whirled about and driven from the room. The door was then firmly shut. Mrs. Hall was near collapse, and her husband was quite certain that spirits were involved in the affair. Lock him out, cried the wife, she should have known all along, with him never going to church, and those goggled eyes, and all bandaged up like that. The blacksmith, Mr. Sandy Wadgers was summoned from nearby, and his expert opinion was that it was doubtless a case of witchcraft. The tobacconist's apprentice was called over to the discussion, which now

turned upon the point of whether to break down the stranger's door
or not. Mr. Wadgers was of the sound opinion that care should be
taken since a door once broken down, you know, can't be unbroken
down, and that was for certain. Suddenly, the stranger's door
opened; and he could be seen descending the stairs, all wrapped up
as he usually was. When he entered the parlor and viciously
slammed the door, it took some encouragement by Wadgers to get
Mr. Hall to go on in and demand an explanation. Hall did so but was
hardly inside when the stranger's voice bellowed at him, and he retreated hastily.

CHAPTER 7
The Unveiling of the Stranger

The stranger had entered the parlor of the Coach and Horses Inn at
about half past five in the morning, and it was now about noon. He
had eaten nothing but had rung his bell furiously. No one, however,
would answer him. With the news of a burglary at the vicarage, the
stranger was immediately suspected, and Mr. Hall and Wadgers
went off to consult Shuckleforth, the magistrate. A crowd now gathered, and some of the younger and hardier ventured to get a look at
the stranger under the drawn window blinds. All that was heard,
however, was an occasional oath, some raging and the smashing of
bottles. Suddenly, he opened the parlor door and was calling for
Mrs. Hall. Where were his meals? Where was the money for his
unpaid bill? was her reply. He might be waiting for receipt of more
funds, but she could not. When he offered to give her something
toward the bill, she questioned how this could be since he had only
recently told her he had nothing on hand. The patrons at the bar
took notice of this as well. And besides, raved Mrs. Hall, there are
some things we should like to know — such as how you come in and
out without using the door and just what it is you've been doing to
my furniture and. . . . Suddenly the stranger roared for silence and
got it. You don't understand, he cried, but I'll show you. His nose,
artificial it was, was flung on the floor along with wrappings and
whiskers. There was a great turmoil, and people came running toward the inn from all over town. Word got about quickly — no head;
he had no head. Soon Wadgers, Hall and Bobby Jaffers, the village
constable, appeared and marched to the parlor where the headless
man was gnawing a crust of bread. As they closed in on the stranger,

Hall received a sound kick in the ribs; and Jaffers, trying to say something about a warrant, grappled with his headless opponent. All at once the stranger declared he would surrender, even though as it seemed, he had the better of the battle. Jaffers wished to use handcuffs, and the invisible man said that his own invisibility was a nuisance but no reason why he should be tormented and poked at by every curious bumpkin. All the while, he seemed to be undoing the buttons of his clothes, with Jaffers insisting on the use of handcuffs. The stranger refused, and suddenly the coat and socks and shoes were flung off as if by magic. Stop him, cried Jaffers; and a great thrashing about ensued in which Henfrey, Jaffers and others received some stout blows. The conflict overflowed into the hall, through the front door, and out into the street. Men staggered right and left. Jaffers went down. A woman across the road screamed as something unseen careened against her. A dog howled, kicked by something invisible. Soon confusion had passed, and panic took hold throughout the village. Jaffers, meanwhile, lay in a heap on the ground.

COMMENT: The invisible man is now a hunted creature. Fear and suspicion of what they did not understand have turned the townspeople to panic and violence. The invisible man's sanctuary in the inn is now gone, and he has been driven out of doors like a wild beast. There will be little, if any, rest or peace for him from now on.

CHAPTER 8
In Transit

On the same day the invisible stranger had engaged in his furious exchange with the people of Iping, a Mr. Gibbins, an amateur naturalist thereabouts, was reclining on the broad open downs outside of town. He was dozing when he distinctly heard the sound of a man coughing, sneezing and swearing. It was almost beside him, but there was no one there. The swearing, moreover, had a range and discrimination not known to an uncultivated man; Mr. Gibbins noted this as the voice trailed off in the direction of Adderdean. He had not heard of the invisible man, as yet, but this remarkable circumstance was enough to send him off at a quick rate toward the town.

CHAPTER 9
Mr. Thomas Marvel

Mr. Thomas Marvel was well worth seeing with his aggressive nose, full and flexible face, vigorously bristling beard, and the frequent appearance of string where buttons and shoelaces should have been. Certainly, he was a bachelor, and something of a tramp. He was seated in a ditch a short distance outside Iping and was contemplating a pair of sturdy boots he was about to try on. They were large for him, and he did not like large boots, but then his own boots were too thin for damp weather. A voice from behind, which did not startle him at all, remarked that at least they were boots. Yes, but such ugly ones, responded Mr. Marvel, not the least disconcerted by the interruption. It has been a good country for boots for ten years, said Marvel, and now such luck. A terrible country said the voice, with pigs for people. Indeed, agreed Mr. Marvel, and, thereupon, looked over his shoulder to see the source of the voice—but there was no one there. The amazed Mr. Marvel looked here and there threatening and raving a bit at what he thought to be a trick of some sort. At last he determined that the drink had been the cause of it, but the mysterious voice quickly corrected this impression and advised him to keep calm. Crazy, cried Thomas Marvel, I must be crazy. No such thing, returned the voice. Imagination, sheer imagination, cried Marvel; and the voice replied that he would fling stones at the disbeliever until he thought otherwise. A stone struck the bewildered tramp's toe, and he howled wildly but calmed down somewhat. I'm invisible, said the voice, an invisible man and that's all there is to understand. At last Thomas Marvel was convinced, but only after he had reached out and touched the invisible man, the arms, face and chest. Marvel had been chosen by the invisible stranger because he suspected that the tramp was an outcast much like himself. Marvel was to do an important job. But if you betray me . . . , said the voice. Never, never, said the terrified Marvel. Just say what's to be done and I'll do it.

CHAPTER 10
Mr. Marvel's Visit to Iping

When the panic in Iping had subsided, a degree of skepticism took hold. People gradually resumed their affairs and the amusements of Whit Monday, and the skeptics made a fair jest of this invisible man. Still, there was a certain tentativeness in the air. Games were played and the children ran their races, but there was the likes of old Fletcher who took a dim view of holiday fun making and spent the day whitewashing the ceiling of his front room.

About four o'clock, a stranger entered town and displayed some rather curious characteristics, such as acting furtively and indulging in a sharp conversation with himself. Mr. Huxter happened to notice him and the strange struggle he seemed to have with himself before entering the Coach and Horses. Once inside, he had tried to enter the parlor but was deterred by Hall. He emerged, still behaving suspiciously, and Mr. Huxter continued to observe him as he made his way into the yard beside the parlor window. Trying to appear casual, he lit a clay pipe and disappeared into the yard. Huxter was about to follow when the stranger emerged with a bundle of books wrapped in a blue tablecloth. Stop thief, cried Huxter, and took off after the man and his parcel. Suddenly, he stumbled over something invisible and sprawled upon the ground in a semiconscious state.

CHAPTER 11
In the Coach and Horses

When Mr. Huxter first spied the curious Mr. Marvel near the inn, Cuss and the Rev. Mr. Bunting were in the parlor of that establishment closely examining the invisible man's possessions. Cuss came up with the stranger's diary which seemed to be written in a mixture of code, mathematical symbols and Greek, a fact which caused Mr. Bunting some awkwardness since he was considered to have some command of Greek. It was then that someone, namely Mr. Marvel, opened the door and inquired if this was the taproom. No, said the occupants somewhat annoyed. "All right," was the response, but strangely enough the voice sounded different from that which had just inquired about the taproom. Cuss then locked the door, and as he did so there was the sound of someone sniffing. As they returned to an examination of the Greek, Mr. Bunting fumbled with his glasses as his face colored somewhat. Suddenly, the vicar was aware of a strong pressure gripping the back of his neck which forced his chin down toward the table. Cuss was in the same situation, and both men became even more astonished as a voice from nowhere reprimanded them for their busy curiosity into private quarters and private possessions. The voice threatened them so that they offered no resistance, and they were informed that the speaker was in need of some clothes since his own were nowhere in evidence in the room.

COMMENT: With the Rev. Mr. Bunting, Wells provides some humorous characterization. Some of the invisible man's notebooks are written in Greek and the vicar is now called upon to demonstrate a knowledge he no longer possesses, or as Wells says, he "had no Greek left in his mind worth talking about. . . ." The vicar coughed, fumbled with his glasses, and ". . . wished something would happen to avert the seemingly inevitable exposure." There is only a brief engagement of Mr. Bunting by Wells but it is a deft and sympathetic stroke of real and animating characterization in a minor figure. It is, moreover, part of Wells's consistent use of the comic throughout the book, providing the proper touch of relief for the mounting suffering and peril that has become the lot of the invisible man.

CHAPTER 12
The Invisible Man Loses His Temper

While Messrs. Cuss and Bunting were being firmly gripped by the invisible man, Mr. Teddy Henfrey and Mr. Hall were in the taproom a few yards away discussing the perplexing events of recent days. From the parlor there came some thumping amid muffled and animated voices. The vicar's voice, somewhat halting, replied to Hall's inquiry about the commotion that everything was fine and please do not interrupt. However, the gentlemen in the taproom were certain that they heard various protests and refusals from within and a cry of "disgraceful." There was the sound also of an opening window. It was about this time that Mr. Huxter out in the street had cried "Stop thief," and had taken after the fleeing form of Mr. Thomas Marvel, only to be tumbled to the ground by some unseen force. Mr. Hall and two laborers from the taproom were quickly out in the street and off in hot pursuit of the galloping Mr. Thomas Marvel. These three gentlemen soon found themselves sprawled upon the ground, having been tripped by something unseen. Mrs. Hall had stayed behind to watch the till and was there to see Mr. Cuss emerge from the parlor, his lower portions wrapped in a cloth of sorts, since the invisible man having passed his diaries out the window to the waiting Thomas Marvel, had made off with Mr. Cuss's trousers and all of the vicar's clothes as well. A crowd of townsfolk which had taken up the pursuit of the invisible man had come upon Hall and the two laborers sprawled about the roadway with no one else in sight and had straightaway turned about and thundered pell mell in the opposite direction, just in time to flatten Teddy Henfrey, who had paused momentarily to minister to the fallen Mr. Huxter. Mr. Henfrey got to his feet and in the midst of the wild rout made directly for the inn. Behind him he heard a loud cry of pain and outrage and the sound of someone struck in the face. The voice of the invisible man was unmistakable, and in a moment Mr. Cuss was on hand shouting that the invisible man was coming back half mad and advising the vicar to save himself. The vicar, who now stood in the parlor clad in hearth rug and newspaper, required little deliberation and was out the window and off down the street as swiftly as his chubby legs would carry him.

It appears now that the invisible man's temper had gotten the best of him, and what had probably been an honest effort to escape became in the end a senseless beating of anyone within reach and the expression of a sheer joy in inflicting pain. The town, therefore, was quite put to rout, and the street was filled with people in panicked flight seeking sanctuary wherever they could from the fury of the man who could not be seen. The invisible man himself continued his terrifying hijinks for a while by smashing every window in the Coach and Horses, tearing up a street lamp and cutting telegraph wires. As suddenly as his fury had been released, he was gone and never again descended upon the thoroughly harassed village of Iping.

COMMENT: Once again it is worth pausing to consider Wells's use of the comic. Here, certainly, is an engaging collection of bungling rustics. The Rev. Mr. Bunting, minus his clothes and his ecclesiastical dignity, provides a comic portrait of an English country parson akin to such classic figures as Parson Adams in Henry Fielding's *Joseph Andrews* or Oliver Goldsmith's Parson Primrose in *The Vicar of Wakefield*. However, in the humorous rout of the town by the invisible man, the reader must not be diverted from this character's torment altogether. It is important to note here that the invisible man has now turned on humanity. His temper, inflammable in the first place, is now something to be reckoned with. When Cuss shouts that the invisible stranger has gone mad, he is not overstating the situation altogether.

CHAPTER 13
Mr. Marvel Discusses His Resignation

By early evening of the same day that Iping was put to flight, a short thick-set man in a well-worn silk hat could be seen making his way along the road to Bramblehurst. He seemed weary and upset and spoke periodically with an unseen voice. At times he appeared to be prodded along by an invisible force. Mr. Marvel was now protesting to his invisible and angry companion that he had not tried to elude him and had simply gotten off on the wrong turn. Mr. Marvel also protested that he was certainly not the man for the work the invisible stranger had in mind. He was not strong. His heart was weak. Furthermore, he was a bungler and had no nerve whatsoever. His arguments were to no avail; and with the invisible man's hand upon his shoulder and the threat of violence hanging over him, Mr. Thomas Marvel proceeded submissively through the streets of the next town they encountered.

CHAPTER 14
At Port Stowe

On the following morning at about ten o'clock, Mr. Marvel was seated on a bench by the inn at Port Stowe. He sat with a parcel of three books beside him, and his manner was most agitated. An old mariner had just emerged from the inn and proceeded to seat himself beside the nervous Mr. Marvel. As he approached, the mariner had distinctly heard the sound of coins being dropped in a pocket. He found the suggestion of wealth rather ill fitting with the threadbare and soiled appearance of Mr. Marvel and paused to pass the time of day and to comment upon the books beside his companion on the bench. The mariner had a newspaper and related to the apprehensive Marvel the most amazing news of an invisible man at Iping. They say he inflicted all sorts of injuries on various townsfolk and had taken the road to Port Stowe—a most astonishing situation it was, and Mr. Marvel was in total agreement about that to be sure. Mr. Marvel was most relieved to learn that there was no mention in the papers that the invisible man had any companion, and with that he began to take the mariner into his confidence. Pausing to listen for a moment, Marvel confessed to knowing something about this invisible man and was about to continue his tale when he was brought up rather short by what seemed to be a spasm of pain. A toothache, he cried, and began to edge his way off the bench. To the protests of the mariner that he had not told what he knew of the invisible man, Mr. Marvel could only cry out—Hoax—all a lie—no invisible man at all. The mariner suddenly took offense at the fact that Marvel had let him talk on about this invisible fellow when he knew about it all the while. An argument ensued, but Marvel could be observed retreating in a most curious manner, in jerky uneven movements, as if hustled along by something unseen. This same startled mariner was to hear that day from the lips of another seagoing man an account of money seen floating through the air and of the receipt of a violent blow when he sought to snatch at it. In fact, sums of money seemed to be snatched up and floated through the air all over Port Stowe that day—and strangely enough they invariably made their way into the pockets of the reluctant Thomas Marvel.

CHAPTER 15
The Man Who Was Running

The young Dr. Kemp sat in his study and admired the lovely sunset visible toward Burdock. However, his attention was taken by the distant figure of a short stocky man in a battered silk hat running towards him fast as he could over the edge of the hill—and he was reminded of the wild fellow who had run into him that day shouting something about an invisible man coming. Dr. Kemp noticed how hard the man ran and what little progress he seemed to be making— as if loaded down with weights. The young doctor turned away, but those nearer the breathless man, Mr. Marvel, noticed the expression of terror and exhaustion on his face, and how he jangled like a great money bag as he ran. He ran like a man possessed, and all whom he passed looked on in amazement. Then, suddenly, there seemed to be a rush of wind, the sound of footsteps and a heavy breathing without any visible source. Just as suddenly, there arose cries that an invisible man was coming; with a great flurry of activity, doors were slammed and bolted as quickly as was humanly possible.

CHAPTER 16
The Jolly Cricketers

At the Jolly Cricketers pub, the battered Marvel burst in with pitiful cries for sanctuary, declaring that the invisible man was close behind. Still clutching the parcel of books, he pleaded to be hidden somewhere, anywhere; for the invisible man had threatened to kill him. There was a heavy beating at the door, and the terrified Mr. Marvel was sheltered behind the bar by the proprietor. An off-duty policeman said he wished he had his truncheon with him, and at that moment the front window was smashed in. A patron with a black beard produced a revolver and called to the policeman to unlock the door and let in whatever was out there. Come in, the bearded man called out. Five minutes later, nothing had happened. Were all the other doors locked? asked Marvel. The barman went to check, returning to announce that the yard door was open and that the fellow might be in the house at that very moment. As the barman announced that he had probed the kitchen with a carving knife and that the invisible man was not there, the bar parlor door was smashed open and the men could hear shrieking from inside where Marvel had gone to hide. As the patrons and the barman rushed in, they saw Marvel crumpled up, struggling, and being dragged into the kitchen by something invisible that had a fast hold on him. The policeman rushed in, grabbed at the invisible man's wrists and was promptly hurled back with a sharp blow in the face. Marvel crawled off as the struggle intensified about him, and the voice of the invisible man could be heard as someone stamped on his foot. A piece of tile whizzed through the air, at which the bearded man produced his revolver once again and let loose a wide spread of five shots towards the doorway and the narrow yard from whence the deadly fragment of tile had come. A lantern was called for, and they all began a search for an invisible body.

CHAPTER 17
Dr. Kemp's Visitor

Dr. Kemp had been writing in his study when he heard the sharp crack of several shots. He went to the window and surmised that the source must have been somewhere near the Cricketers as he could see a crowd gathering there. Gazing out over the town, his mind became lost in a reverie and speculation about possible social conditions in the future and finally turning to a consideration of the dimension of time. He pulled himself up short, closed the window and returned to his writing. The doorbell rang, but the housemaid advised him that it must have been a prank — no one was there.

When he had completed his work about two o'clock in the morning, Dr. Kemp ventured downstairs to pour himself a whisky. Recrossing the hall, he noticed a curious stain on the floor. It appeared to be dried blood. Puzzled, he went upstairs to discover blood on the doorknob of his room, on his bed too, and that the sheet on his bed had been violently torn. Dr. Kemp was a man of science, a nonbeliever in voices, but suddenly there was a voice out of thin air saying, "Good Heavens — Kemp," — and a blood-soaked bandage of torn sheet simply hanging in the air before him. The voice spoke again, and Kemp was hard put not to believe it was simply a trick. An invisible hand touched him and said, "Steady, Kemp, steady," but Kemp instinctively struggled with the invisible force before him as the voice pleaded that it needed help badly. They rolled and fought about the bed with the invisible man shouting that he was Griffin from University College, that he was real but invisible. Remember me, he cried, younger than yourself, almost an albino, well built, with red eyes and a pink and white face? Remember?—I won the chemistry medal.

Kemp collected his wits. It's horrible, he said. The invisible man asked for whisky. Invisibility? Impossible, said Kemp; why only today I proved. . . . The invisible man interrupted and asked for food and clothing and Dr. Kemp obliged. Now wearing a dressing gown, the strange guest gnawed wildly at the food and drank whisky, explaining as he did how a confederate of his had made off with his money and how some fool he had never seen before shot wildly in an effort to bring him down—hence the bloody wrist. Quite a stain on the floor, said the invisible man; the blood becomes visible as it coagulates. What luck to have come upon you, said the visitor, and he puffed one of his host's cigars avidly.

Kemp pressed his guest for information about this invisibility, but the wrist was painful, and the invisible man was feverish and spoke disconnectedly of Thomas Marvel. I should have killed the wretch, he cried; but his fury soon abated, and he was suddenly interested only in sleep. I should not want to be discovered here, said the voice, and then caught himself, realizing that he had just put the idea in Kemp's head.

COMMENT: Wells is now beginning to fill in the background of the invisible man. We know now that his name is Griffin, that he is educated, and that he is an accomplished chemist. He has stumbled upon an old acquaintance from his university days, a man of science with whom he feels a certain professional kinship, one to whom he can relate the nature of his strange experiments in invisibility. Wells, of course, was himself a man of science; and as we have already seen in the Introduction to this book, he won a scholarship to the Royal College of Science where he was privileged to study under the renowned Thomas Henry Huxley. Here there is a touch of the autobiographical, something of Wells's own history taken from the past, reshaped and fitted into the background of the invisible man. It has been English literature's good fortune that the trained precision of the scientific mind has been happily combined in Wells with lively and original imaginative faculties.

CHAPTER 18
The Invisible Man Sleeps

The invisible man took great precautions to see that the doors and windows of the bedroom were secure. He warned Dr. Kemp about possible betrayal, but Kemp gave his word on the matter. Alone outside the locked bedroom, Dr. Kemp meditated on the possibility of becoming invisible. There are invisible creatures in the sea, he thought, and what if a man were made of glass? It would be possible then. He smoked, thought deeply, and then reached for the newspapers that lay nearby. There it was—Iping panic and fright, village gone mad, people injured, incoherent, the vicar, smashed windows. He's mad, thought Kemp—and homicidal, as well. He stayed awake through the remainder of the night and in the morning eagerly perused the latest paper. There was the rest of it—the rout at the Jolly Cricketers, Marvel's account and the business of the money. Mad, said Kemp, a maniac. But would it be a betrayal if I. . . . No, he concluded. He's capable of anything, violent and dangerous. With that he scribbled off a note to Colonel Adye at Port Burdock. He read it, tore it up and wrote another, read it and addressed it. Overhead he heard the invisible man awaken, violently and obviously in a fierce mood.

CHAPTER 19
Certain First Principles

Dr. Kemp advised his guest that the news of his antics was all through the papers, and together they sat down to breakfast with the invisible man somewhat calmed and more willing to relate his tale. At twenty-two he had given up medicine for physics, fascinated, he said, by light and optical density. He had discovered a formula involving pigments and refractions and concerned with four dimensions. And it was all in those three books the tramp Marvel had made off with—miracles, astounding discoveries. What the invisible man had done was to reduce the refractive characteristics of solid and liquid substances to that of air—if something does not reflect or absorb light, it becomes invisible. Certainly, added the voice, the fibers of living creatures are no more opaque than water is. Yes, said Kemp, and only last night I was thinking of the invisibility of certain creatures in water—jellyfish, for example. Then, said the invisible man, alone in my laboratory, it all came together. The pigment in blood could be rendered colorless and human tissue could be made invisible—a man could become invisible—I could be invisible. The disadvantages never struck me then, he said. After all, a poor cramped little instructor in an insignificant college. And a prodding professor, always after him to publish this thing he was working on. There was no money, of course, and the experiments could not continue. He then stole money from his father. But it was not his father's money, Griffin was disgraced, and the older man was driven to suicide.

CHAPTER 20
At The House in Great Portland Street

Kemp did not respond immediately to what the invisible man had told him. Then he advised him to sit and rest, while Kemp was careful to place himself between his guest and the nearest window. The invisible man continued his tale. During the previous December, he had taken lodgings in a shabby London rooming house near Great Portland Street. He had gone to his father's funeral, had felt no sorrow for him and had left his character soiled even in death. He had been a sentimental old man, and that was that. Once in his rooms he felt alive again, surrounded by the experimental equipment purchased with the stolen money.

But we must get those books back, the invisible man suddenly cried to Kemp. It's all written down there. Just as suddenly he returned to his tale and described the way he had experimented at first with pieces of wool and then with a cat belonging to a drunken old woman lodger who had suspected him of experimenting with animals. The cat vanished—all except for the claws and a chemical substance at the back of the eyes. And so, he continued, somewhere there is an invisible cat prowling about.

On the morning before becoming invisible, he had walked about wearily. There had been four years of investigations, but now he dreamed of the numberless advantages of invisibility. He had then gone home, eaten, taken some strychnine to restore himself and had slept. Strychnine, replied Kemp, a devil of a thing! The invisible man continued. He had awakened to a knock at the door, refreshed but extremely irritable. It was the landlord inquiring about the old woman's complaints. Was he experimenting with cats? It was a respectable house, and he would have none of it. Angered, Griffin hastened out with his notebooks and had them sent to a general postal address. He returned to his rooms to complete his experiment in invisibility. On that very evening, it was done. He took drugs to eliminate color from his blood, and about that time the landlord arrived with a notice of eviction. One look at his tenant's face sent him off down the stairs in howls and shrieks. He had seen a face stark white, no longer colored by the pigment of the body's blood. During that night, Griffin experienced great pain but gradually became almost invisible. He then arose and completed the necessary processes as he heard several voices in the hall. The landlord returned with his two stepsons. They beat upon the door, and he answered them simply to provide more time. He heaped papers, straw and packing materials in the entrance of the room, turned on the gas and hunted feverishly for matches. He could find none for the moment, and the three men were smashing in a door panel and breaking open the stout fastenings he had applied to insure privacy. Griffin hastily stepped out the window to a ledge and there observed the amazement as the intruders discovered the room to be empty. The three men, the drunken old woman and a neighbor from across the hall debated spiritedly about the precise character of his work. He slipped back into the room, smashed several instruments and, amid the consternation that this caused, invisibly made his way out the door. When the mystified landlord and his party had left, the invisible man returned to his room, turned on the gas, and set the building ablaze. Out on the street once more, Griffin was dizzy with the plans and opportunities that lay before him.

COMMENT: This chapter is significant not simply for its exposition of the invisible man's own history, but for the fact that it reveals certain peculiar aspects of his character. He had stolen money from his father, money that was not the father's, and then allowed the guilt to remain on the father's head even after suicide. Untouched by natural affection and grief for his father, Griffin had rationalized that the old man was sentimental, soft. It should be noted also that he obviously takes drugs. The strychnine invigorated but simultaneously made him sharp and irritable. There is reason to believe then that some of his violent conduct may be rooted in self-prescribed drugs or stimulants. We have seen evidence of his great temper, violent moods and responses, and there is increasing evidence of madness. Kemp's diagnosis of "homicidal" may not be far from wrong. In addition, the casualness with which Griffin set fire to his rooming house seems to tie in with the coldness and dispassion he felt toward his dead father — a sense of proportion, a conscience and the pangs of a haunting guilt are absent. In the coldness of his scientific objectivity, his humanity has suffered dearly.

CHAPTER 21
In Oxford Street

Griffin's first trial of his invisibility in public was rather awkward and painful for him. He was run into by a man with a basket of soda-water syphons. He was hurt but responded capriciously by swinging the basket about in the air. A cabman nearby grabbed for the basket, struck the invisible man by the ear and a commotion ensued. A crowd gathered and Griffin had all he could do to slip away undetected. He moved with the crowd along Oxford street only to have his feet stepped on. He took to the gutter, but it was rough on his feet as well. He was struck by a hansom cab and splattered with freezing mud from the road. He was stark naked and shivering badly. Invisibly he rode in the hansom, wondering now just how to escape from this situation in which he had gotten himself, when suddenly he had to leap out to avoid a woman who had hailed the cab. In doing so he just avoided being run over by a railway van. With the worst of luck haunting him, Griffin's muddy footprints were noticed as he stopped to allow a Salvation Army band and followers pass. Two children had noticed and a small crowd quickly gathered and followed him. He leaped over a low railing, and the footprints seemed to hustle off by themselves. Griffin had run up streets and around corners and had eluded them at last. He was bruised and sore in a number of places, and every dog he passed sniffed after him energetically. Some people came running along the street, and Griffin observed that his old lodgings were ablaze. Everything that was behind him had been burned — except his checkbook and the three precious volumes of notes that had been sent from Great Portland Street. As the invisible man paused in his story, Kemp seemed agitated as he glanced from the window but encouraged his strange guest to continue.

COMMENT: The blessings of invisibility imagined by Griffin have proved to be a nightmare in reality. The total freedom he foresaw has become an endless threat of danger and injury. Ironically, his invisibility has drawn attention to him. Dogs sniff at a thing they cannot see and passersby, spying footprints that march off by themselves, pursue him eagerly. Like a child let loose in a candy shop, the invisible man has quickly tired of his incredible freedom and has discovered what an insuperable burden it really is.

CHAPTER 22
In the Emporium

So it was that in January, with snow in the air, Griffin began his new life. It was cold and he realized that falling snow would certainly betray him. He had to find shelter, clothing, and warmth—and quickly. It occurred to him that he should go to one of the large department stores where he might hide until closing and then steal food and clothing at will. At Omniums he gained entry and hid among the bedding until the closing hour. In the darkened store, Griffin located the clothing department and there outfitted himself, choosing warm garments and a slouch hat with a downturned brim. In the refreshment area, he ate and drank and then prowled about until he discovered some artificial noses in the toy department—an artificial nose was precisely what he required. This done, he slept upon a heap of down quilts, but that sleep was disturbed by dreams of his father's funeral, the drone of the clergyman, and the sensation of being forced down into the open grave. In the morning he awakened at the opening of the emporium. As he sat up, fully clothed, he was seen by clerks who immediately gave chase. He ran frantically, struck one of his pursuers with a chair, and ran up the stairs, shattering an art pot on the head of another employee. A cook from the refreshment area took up the chase and was rendered inactive with a fiercely swung lamp. The invisible man, now visible with clothing on, tore wildly at the garments until they were strewn about the floor and he had withdrawn into the comparative safety of his former invisibility. At about eleven o'clock, having eluded and bewildered his pursuers, Griffin despaired of the emporium and made his way into the street with absolutely no plan of action in mind.

CHAPTER 23
In Drury Lane

It was an awful situation, continued the invisible man. Even the act of eating would betray me since the unassimilated food would be visible. Snow, rain or fog were all dangerous for me, as well, since each would contribute to partial visibility. Dirt, too, could make me visible and was a constant threat to my safety, he said. He had then decided to locate a theatrical costume shop where he could certainly obtain an artificial nose and some disguise. On the way he collided with a pedestrian and nearly fell under the wheels of a passing cab. He rested in the Covent Garden Market but had to move on, for he had caught a fresh cold and feared his sneezing would betray him. At last he found the shop, a dirty little affair near Drury Lane. He entered, planning to steal any money he could in the bargain. The owner, a short hunched man emerged at the sound of the jangling shop bell and was angered when he saw no one in sight. The shop-keeper heard Griffin's footstep, stopped short and looked about the room. In the meantime the invisible intruder slipped past him into the inner apartment. The man soon followed and resumed the break-fast he had been eating, much to the agony of the hungry Griffin. When the man finished his meal, he took the dishes to the kitchen. Griffin was cold and proceeded to put some coals on the fire, the sound of which brought the hunched proprietor back at a dash. Moving about the house the shopkeeper's acute hearing constantly picked up the sounds of the invisible man just behind or very near him—and once he shouted a half threat to anyone who might be in the house. In one room the invisible man discovered some old clothes and his rummaging again produced his host, this time with an angry look and a revolver. The door to the room was then bolted with the invisible Griffin on the inside. An additional noise by Grif-fin brought the man back once more, and this time he was startled when he happened to touch his invisible intruder. Rats, he said, but he was obviously frightened.

When the little man began moving about the house locking each door and pocketing the keys, Griffin acted and struck him into un-consciousness with a blow on the head, trussed him up, and wrapped him in a sheet. Dr. Kemp protested at this disclosure, but Griffin maintained the necessity of the act under such abnormal cir-cumstances. Roaming about the house, Griffin ate bread and cheese and drank brandy. He selected a mask, some whiskers, a nose, and wrapped himself in some scarfs. He studied himself carefully in a mirror and then with money located in the house ventured out into the world, never once giving thought to the unconscious shopkeep-er, bound tightly and enclosed in a sheet. The invisible man now felt powerful. He could do whatever he wished and could take money whenever and wherever he chose to. He entered a restau-rant, ordered a fine meal, and left in frustration and anger when he realized that he could not eat without exposing his invisible face.

The absurdity of his invisibility soon struck him. What possible good were all the dreamed-of advantages if they could never be enjoyed.

Griffin seemed to glance at the window, and Kemp quickly encouraged him to go on and to explain how it was that he went to Iping. He had gone there, he explained, to work out the process of his change back to visibility, to be used at a time when he finally chose to use it. He had gotten his checkbook and his notebooks and was ready to work. The snow, however, was a constant danger to his pasteboard nose.

Kemp advised him that the papers said he had killed no one in Iping, but Griffin remarked laughingly that there was always that tramp, Marvel, to be dealt with. What fury a man can be capable of, said Griffin. To have worked so long and then have some silly dunce bungle the whole business for you — it's maddening, and I shall go wild if I run into any more of it, he added.

> **COMMENT:** This chapter contains some genuinely humorous parts but as in much of the novel, Wells positions the comic beside unmistakably vicious and indifferent traits in Griffin's character. The hunched shopkeeper bound up and forgotten on an upstairs floor of his shop is reminiscent of the indifference and callousness Griffin displayed at his father's death and the wanton burning of the rooming house. He acts without remorse or conscience and is extremely dangerous. Griffin is a brilliant scientist, but he is most surely mad, or certainly on the very brink of it.

CHAPTER 24
The Plan That Failed

Kemp glanced from the window and wished the three men making their way toward the house would hurry. He returned his attention to Griffin and asked him what he was up to when heading for Port Burdock. The invisible man had planned to leave the country, to go to Spain or Algiers where it was warm and a man might remain invisible and still live. But that swine Marvel with my books, cried Griffin; if I could just lay hold of him. Kemp revealed that Marvel was now in the town jail, put there at his own request for safety's sake. Kemp continued to talk, listening for the sounds of footsteps downstairs. This business of invisibility, Griffin broke in, is particularly useful for killing. Not indiscriminate killing, mind you, but planned and purposeful killing; that is the thing. A reign of terror, you see, said Griffin, laid upon some town like Port Burdock. Terrorize. Obey an invisible man's orders or be killed, he cried. Don't go on alone, suggested Kemp, rambling on and stalling as best he could. Take the world into your confidence. Footsteps, cried Griffin suddenly. Traitor! Traitor! Kemp raced to the door, opened it and shoved back the invisible man, who was hastily disrobing. The door slammed but the key fell to the floor, and Kemp could not retrieve it swiftly enough to prevent Griffin from forcing the door partway open. They struggled. The door burst open. Kemp was hurled to the floor with Griffin's robe heaped on top of him.

Colonel Adye had been ascending the staircase during the struggle. He saw Kemp fall and was himself suddenly struck violently and hurled down to the first floor landing. He could hear a commotion back in the hall, with the two officers who had accompanied him, and then heard the front door slam shut violently. That really does it, cried Kemp, as he descended the stairs battered and bloody. He's gotten free.

> **COMMENT:** Griffin's madness is all too evident in this chapter. What had been curious dreaming about an extraordinary freedom coupled with invisibility has now become a maniacal drive to terrorize and kill, to strike fear into humanity. This seems almost a defensive response on Griffin's part. He has had an agonizing time of it and has come to interpret man's understandable reactions to invisibility as hateful stupidity and clumsiness. His response is violent and a reign of terror on his part is almost totally comprised of spite and revenge. Beneath it all is a mind twisted into homicidal imbalance, impulsively violent and wildly obsessed now with the notion of self-preservation.

CHAPTER 25
The Hunting of the Invisible Man

For a moment, in his dazed condition, all that Dr. Kemp could communicate to Colonel Adye was the fact that the invisible man was mad. Certainly he would kill and injure without remorse. They were in complete agreement; he must be caught, and quickly. Those books of his would keep him in the neighborhood, but he must be routed out, kept from food and sleep, driven into the cold and rain of the night. All doors must be bolted, all weapons hidden away. And on the roads, Kemp added, with some hesitation, powdered glass. It's cruel, he confessed, but he is mad, totally inhuman.

> **COMMENT:** "He has cut himself off from his kind. His blood be upon his own head." With these words of Kemp's Wells concludes Chapter 25. They are in fact a judgment of doom upon Griffin, the verdict of his fellow men that he be hunted down like an animal. Deprived of comforts and driven into the violent elements, he is to be run down with bloodhounds. Griffin is now an outcast, an alien among his own species.

CHAPTER 26
The Wicksteed Murder

In racing wildly from Kemp's house, the invisible man had knocked aside a small child playing nearby, breaking its ankle. Until about half past two in the afternoon, nothing was known of his whereabouts. During that interval Kemp's betrayal preyed upon Griffin's mind. He raged at the thought of it, treachery from the one in whom he had confided.

The countryside had come alive to action as soon as word of his escape and presence thereabouts spread. Every precaution was taken. All who had no purpose out of doors bolted their entries from the inside while armed citizens in small bands and mounted policemen roamed about. In the afternoon a Mr. Wicksteed, a steward to Lord Burdock, had his fatal encounter with the invisible man. It seems that the murder was done with an iron rod, Mr. Wicksteed having been beaten savagely, almost beyond recognition. A child reported seeing the victim trotting along at a curious gait pursuing and striking out at something invisible that seemed to be just ahead of him. It appears then that Wicksteed's murder may not have been altogether unprovoked and it was already known what a fierce temper Griffin had. Furthermore two men near Fern Bottom reported a wailing, sobbing voice, shouting occasionally, that passed near them and moved off toward the hill.

That afternoon Griffin's hate for Kemp must have deepened profoundly as he recollected that his very confessions were now being used in an effort to apprehend him. Somewhere, however, he must have slept and obtained food; for on the following morning, the vileness of his temper and his great physical strength had returned. It was to be his last great confrontation with humanity.

CHAPTER 27
The Siege of Kemp's House

The note Kemp received was wild and almost irrational in its belligerence and hysteria: It was the beginning of a new age; the Reign of the Terror was to commence; Port Burdock was now under *his* control — the Terror; Kemp's reward was to be death; no cleverness in hiding would prevent it; the game was beginning; death was coming; death for Kemp.

Kemp considered the letter. If Griffin wanted a game, that's what it would be; but Kemp would be the bait. Kemp went to the window and heard a sharp rapping — it must have been a sparrow, he thought, but he remained nervous. When the doorbell rang, it was Colonel Adye announcing that Kemp's servant, who had been sent off with some letters, one to Adye, had been assaulted. As the men talked the sound of broken glass came from above. It was the invisible man smashing the windows with stones. This is the beginning, said Kemp. Adye would go for bloodhounds. He asked Kemp if he had a revolver. Kemp hesitated, and then ashamed of the pause, handed over the one he had in his pocket. A ground floor window smashed, and with that Adye slipped through the doorway and was off. As he moved towards the gate, a voice halted him. Adye gripped the revolver. Back to the house, commanded the voice. A struggle ensued and the gun was wrested from the Colonel. There was little choice involved now, and Adye walked back toward the door with the puzzled Kemp watching him from the house. Suddenly Adye whirled, lunged for the gun, missed, and fell to earth as a light puff of blue smoke curled and lifted upward in the afternoon air. There soon began a furious banging and ringing at the door. Kemp remained still and his servants, by command, had locked themselves in their rooms. In the distance were the housemaid who had been attacked by Griffin and two policemen. Their pace was agonizingly slow for Dr. Kemp. From the direction of the kitchen came the thunderous sounds of smashing and splintering wood. Kemp went to the door and peered in. The iron fastening on the shutters literally exploded, and Kemp beheld a wildly swung axe seemingly suspended in air and chopping away at what remained of the window frame and the iron across it. Suddenly, a shot was fired at him—a near miss. He locked the kitchen door, but Griffin chopped away furiously. The two policemen arrived with the maid, just in time to engage the invisible Griffin and his axe. One policeman struck out sharply with a poker Kemp had handed him and knocked the revolver from the invisible man's hand. One officer was struck in the head with the axe but a simultaneous blow from the poker struck home on Griffin who cried out in intense pain. With the sound of fast moving feet, the invisible man was gone—and, as a matter of fact, so was Dr. Kemp. A hero, said one policeman, clearing his head and rising to his feet. The second officer resorted to somewhat stronger language in his appraisal of the absent doctor.

CHAPTER 28
The Hunter Hunted

Mr. Heelas was Dr. Kemp's neighbor and simply did not believe all this invisible man nonsense. He was walking in his garden, unperturbed, when he happened to notice how battered Dr. Kemp's house appeared. He was even more astonished to see Dr. Kemp's maid coming out through a window with the good doctor directly behind her. Kemp ran and stumbled along at a great rate, crouched as if not wanting to be seen. Straight for Mr. Heelas' house he came as the household flew into an instant hubbub. Mr. Heelas bolted the doors and windows and would not admit the doctor who had just raced through his yard in a great devastation of the asparagus beds. No, said Mr. Heelas, you can't come in. I don't care if he's after you— and suddenly Mr. Heelas had become a believer in the invisible man. Kemp fled to the hill road with Griffin close behind him, as was evidenced by another trampling of Mr. Heelas' asparagus, this time by invisible feet. The road was deserted, and the houses along it were shut tight. Kemp ran faster; he was certain he could hear footsteps close behind him. Soon he was down into town running past the Jolly Cricketers, which was diligently locking up too. He decided to try for the police station. People still on the streets stared curiously at his wild pace. Laborers popped their heads up out of ditches to watch Kemp racing past. His run broke for a moment but quickly picked up again as he heard footsteps behind. He changed his mind about the police station and made for an alley. Suddenly, behind him he was aware of other running feet, those of the townsfolk. Men and women, a train conductor and a huge laborer were thundering along. "He's over here," cried Kemp as the crowd descended. All at once Kemp was struck in the face by an invisible fist.

He fell to the ground, and there were suddenly fingers about his throat, but with a certain weakness now. In a moment the giant laborer stood over Kemp and the invisible Griffin. Down came a heavy shovel; there was a groan and a sickening thud as the implement found its mark. The invisible man was held down firmly but the effort was wasted. He was dead. Gradually, however, the people who had gathered noticed the outline of a human shape beginning to form. In a short time the body of Griffin had become visible once again; and they saw him in his pitiful and battered condition, a young man of about thirty, an albino, his face distorted and his eyes shining like garnets. When a sheet was brought out, he was covered and carried into the Jolly Cricketers.

COMMENT: Somehow the final victory over the invisible man seems a hollow one. Lying there in the street, visible once more, he is more pitiful than terrible. His great torment and suffering seem more real now. Here are the remains of a twisted and maddened human, driven to destruction by the perverted brilliance of his own mind: Griffin, the alien, the outcast, feared, hunted and finally killed. He had reached into the unknown areas of science, and the unknown has always frightened man. He was brilliant, but his humanity was frail, and he could not maintain his discovery in proper perspective.

Wells allows us to sympathize with Griffin. He is mad and remorseless, but his fellow men are no help. Kemp too pays for his betrayal; and it must strike the reader as appropriately ironic that Kemp, the hunter and betrayer, is himself pursued and denied sanctuary as the invisible man was. Ironic, too, is the fact that the shutting of the houses and shops was his own idea. Kemp is a good man, but with a sense of justice Wells allows him to taste for a while some of the pain and terror that the invisible Griffin had known constantly.

THE EPILOGUE

It seems that near Port Stowe there is a small inn called The Invisible Man, operated as it were by a short portly little man with a thrusting nose and a rather rosy complexion. If you drink well and deeply at his establishment, he will be more than willing to tell you about all that happened to him. Those lawyers had tried their best to do him out of the money found on him, but they simply couldn't prove just who owned what. And besides that, he'd even been paid a guinea for every time he related his adventures at the music hall. But he always maintains that the invisible man made off with the notebooks, and it's Dr. Kemp's fault for spreading about that he had them. After this remark, Mr. Thomas Marvel usually displays considerable nervousness.

Mr. Marvel is a man of bachelor tastes, even now retaining the use of string in the support of his trousers—although he has substituted buttons in the more visible and becoming places. He is even considered a man of wisdom, a profound thinker, and one who has an extraordinary knowledge of the roads throughout the south of England.

On Sunday mornings, though, when the inn is closed, he will invariably draw a measure of gin for himself, unlock a particular cupboard, and lay out before him three worn volumes. He will handle them appreciatively, then examine the curious symbols and marks on the pages. He fixes his eyes upon the contents and ignorantly mumbles some approximation of what he sees before him. Marvelous, he says, marvelous secrets here right enough. What a one for brains he was, mutters Thomas Marvel. Once I just get the hang of all this, then . . . oh then! Mr. Marvel soon permits his mind the luxury of a great daydream, visions that play before his mind's eye. And yet, despite all the inquisition and the careful investigations of Colonel Adye and Dr. Kemp, those volumes of rare secrets have never been discovered in the locked cupboard of The Invisible Man inn.

CHARACTER ANALYSIS

THE INVISIBLE MAN: Griffin had been a brilliant young chemist and researcher, confined and unappreciated as an instructor in a small English college. His brilliance had led him to investigations in physics and the properties of light. It is interesting to observe that as his passion for experiment and his devotion to pure scientific investigations accelerated, there was a companion deterioration of his conscience and sense of morality. Nothing was important enough to stand in his way. When he required money to advance his experiments in invisibility, he stole it from his father. It was not the father's money, and the result was suicide and burial in disgrace. Griffin suffered neither remorse nor grief, and yet the roots of guilt were there, for in his dreams he pictured himself thrown into this father's grave and buried along with him.

Griffin was quick to anger, due perhaps to a naturally irascible disposition, but aggravated to a degree, it seems, by the taking of drugs and stimulants. What may have begun as quick temper and impatience rapidly deteriorated into violent rage and a homicidal bent. Madness, too, appears to have set in, but its causes are several. Griffin's deterioration is self-induced to a considerable extent, but his alienation from his own kind is greatly assisted by other human beings. Fear and superstition follow him, and it is often a defensive mechanism of the human species to lash out and destroy that which it fears and does not understand. Griffin's alienation becomes complete, and society hunts him down as it would an animal, finally beating to death this invisible monstrosity.

Is the guilt all Griffin's? Wells does not treat his character in a totally cold manner. Griffin is brilliant, but he has brought a grandly naive quality to his dreams of invisibility. He is rather harshly and painfully restored to a sense of reality as he is chased by dogs, hunted down in a department store, nearly run over in the streets, and constantly subjected to the discomfort of exposure and the affliction of head colds. He is a man caught in a trap of his own making, but his situation is aggravated by frequent accidents and misunderstanding. Then, of course, he is betrayed by the only person in whom he placed confidence. Perhaps it was Dr. Kemp's duty to report a man whom he was convinced was a homicidal maniac. Still, the reader cannot help but sympathize somewhat with Griffin in his wild unreasoning desire for vengeance and his keen sense of having been betrayed by a friend and fellow man of science. Griffin's end is tragic, but it is the culmination of the tragic course he had followed since he first ventured into the unknown terrors of invisibility.

DR. KEMP: Griffin feels a bond with Kemp because they had attended the same university together and are both men of science. Dr. Kemp, however, has never allowed the scientist's necessary objectivity to overwhelm his own humanity as is the case with Griffin. Kemp is down to earth and, while perhaps not possessing Griffin's inventive genius, has maintained a sense of balance. Kemp, of course, is not a violent man, and he is quick to detect that Griffin's erratic and mercurial temper is a potentially dangerous thing. We may wince somewhat at his betrayal of Griffin; the reader instinctively cheers the underdog, but Kemp's concern is for the violence and harm this dangerous man may do to others. At this point he is a potential murderer, and the trust and confidence he places in Kemp only make that doctor's betrayal of that faith all the more difficult to accomplish in good conscience.

As a literary creation Kemp is important technically for he acts as something of a foil for Griffin's fury. He is the opposite side of the coin, a balancing device for Griffin's excessiveness.

CONTRAST IN SCIENTIFIC TYPES: In Kemp and Griffin, Wells dramatizes two different types of scientific approach. Griffin is a throwback to the medieval alchemist, who sought scientific truth for secret, private power; in this sense, Griffin is the early Faustian scientist. Kemp is the modern researcher who publishes his own findings and expects to share in the discoveries of other scientists: concerned with the advancement not of self but of human knowledge, he is the Baconian scientist.

THE WAR OF THE WORLDS

"But who shall dwell in these worlds if they be
inhabited? . . . Are we or they Lords of the World?
. . . And how are all things made for Man?"

Johann Kepler (1571–1630)

BOOK I
THE COMING OF THE MARTIANS

CHAPTER 1
The Eve of the War

In the complacency of the latter part of the nineteenth century, there
was no one who would believe that man and his earth were being
closely observed from space by beings as mortal as man, but with
intelligence far superior to his. Men speculated on the possibilities
of life on Mars, but those creatures they imagined might exist there
were always inferior to themselves. Yet man was even then being
watched and planned against, and in the early twentieth century
there was an incredible awakening for humanity. But man is so blind
and so vain that by the end of the nineteenth century, there was no
writer who had conceived of the idea of intelligent life on Mars. After all, their planet is older than the earth. Its physical condition is a
mystery; and yet it should be realized that if it is older than earth, it
is also nearer its own end as well. The great cooling process that
must someday come to our planet is already advanced there. Necessity, then, may have prompted them to gaze out into space with
instruments beyond our conception and fix their attention and hopes
upon earth, still warm and green and fertile. It surely must be that
from their planet they looked upon us much as we regard those creatures here on earth so far inferior to our own intelligence. In considering their assault upon the earth, we must be reserved in our judg-

ments; for have we not in our way been equally as cruel and heartless to our own kind on many occasions? Are we then so endowed with the spirit of compassion and mercy that we can point at the Martians so accusingly?

The Martians must have calculated their invasion long and well, and their mathematical proficiencies must certainly be far superior to ours. In 1894 a brilliant light was observed emanating from Mars. It seems reasonable that this brightness occurred while they were casting the great gun from which their space projectiles were hurled at us. It was six years ago that the assault began. From an observatory in Java had come word of a great flame-out of incandescent gas from Mars, hydrogen mostly, according to the spectroscope. The mass of flaming gas then moved at tremendous velocity toward the earth. The papers hardly noticed the event, so awesome in its foreshadowing of terrors to come; and the world went about its daily rounds. However, I had met the renowned astronomer Ogilvy, and he was most excited about the phenomenon. Together we kept vigil at the observatory at Ottershaw. Through the telescope one could look out into a void of forty million miles between earth and the Red Planet of War, forty million miles through which was hurtling a thing beyond man's wildest dreams. That night, some twenty-four hours after the first burst of gaseous flame from the planet, another occurred, and unknown to us, another Martian missile was then on its way to earth. On the way home, Ogilvy scoffed at the romantic notion of an inhabitated Mars and speculated that the distant planet might well be receiving a shower of meteors. There were stupendous odds he'd said against human life on Mars—but despite his assurances, there occurred an additional burst of flame from the planet on each of the succeeding ten nights. The papers, the cartoonists, did notice and comment upon these distant phenomena. However, men went about their business as usual, little suspecting or caring about the grim fate that roared toward them from space with each passing hour. For my own part, I was much involved in learning to ride a bicycle and in the preparation of some papers on the development of moral concepts in relation to the civilization's advancement. That night I went for a stroll with my wife and, as we passed some joyous partygoers, the world seemed so much at peace—and the dangers from space somewhat unreal.

COMMENT: In Wells the compatibility of science and good narrative fiction is assured. In his hands, the implausible and the improbable become distinctly possible. In this opening chapter, the author, as the narrator, creates a sensation of time running out for earth as people blissfully and complacently carry on their duties and diversions while a hideous reign of terror is at that very moment descending upon them from space. Man seems weak and shallow here, petty and pitiful beside the great intelligences that have calculated the forthcoming invasion of earth. Even the narrator is busy with his bicycle and is not totally exempted from the category of complacency. He is at work also on treatises concerning the moral elements in society. Somehow the topic, which is certainly the voice of Wells and his social moral consciousness, seems futile and belated in the face of what is to come — and this is certainly part of Wells's intention here.

CHAPTER 2
The Falling Star

On the night that the first projectile struck earth, I had been in my study working. Many must have seen it flash across the sky and must have taken it for an ordinary meteor. Certainly Ogilvy did. He believed that it struck near the sandpits on the common between Horsell, Ottershaw and Woking. Soon after dawn, he did indeed locate it where it had plunged into sand and clay, and lay mostly buried. Ogilvy found himself alone with the thing. He approached it cautiously and observed its massive cylindrical shape and the ashy clinkers that began to drop off from the nose of the object. Despite the great heat, he moved closer and to his astonishment observed that the circular top of the cylinder was slowly rotating. The flashes on Mars and this red hot cylinder immediately linked up in his mind, and he imagined someone within was trying desperately to make his way out. He attempted to assist in the unscrewing of the cylinder top but was repelled by the dull radiation. All at once, he made off for Woking. He ran wildly, unable to make passersby understand what he had found. He then chanced upon Henderson, a London journalist. He made him understand, and the two men hurried back to the spot where the Martian thing lay. They rapped upon the cylinder and with no response forthcoming raced excitedly back to town. By eight o'clock in the morning some townsolk were on their way to the common to see the Martians whom everyone was certain had perished. When I heard the news I lost no time in getting across the Ottershaw bridge and out to the sandpits.

CHAPTER 3
On Horsell Common

At the spot where the thing had plunged to earth, a group of some twenty people had assembled. The thing was colossal in bulk and was embedded in the ground amid charred earth and gravel. About the object, on the edge of the spot, sat young boys, various unemployed, the town gardener and butcher, and several chronic idlers. I studied it as closely as I could and perceived that the gray scale upon the thing was no ordinary oxide and that the yellowish-white metal that appeared between the cylinder and its lid was thoroughly unfamiliar. Certainly, the thing could be called extraterrestrial—a term that would have been totally without meaning to those curious souls that hung about the pit. The early editions of the evening papers made hay of the whole business. They spoke of a message from Mars and the extraordinary occurence at Woking and startled London with their headlines. At the pit itself were Henderson, Ogilvy and Stent, the Astronomer Royal. With them were several workmen with spades and pickaxes. Ogilvy called me down into the pit when he spied me; and when I scrambled down there, I could see that the cylinder had cooled considerably, allowing the workmen to uncover a large portion of it. I was asked to contact Lord Hilton and request some railing or such to keep the crowds back. I was told also that something was audible from within the object, but that the men were not able to unscrew the top. At Lord Hilton's, I was told he was expected by the six o'clock train; and so I had tea and walked to the station to meet him.

CHAPTER 4
The Cylinder Opens

When I returned to the pit and the Martian spaceship, the crowd had increased noticeably, and the cone of the thing had unscrewed even more. The crowd pushed forward, and the cone continued to loosen until it finally fell off and onto the gravel. There was movement from within; and, gradually, what seemed to be tentacles uncoiled from the opening, sending a shudder of panic and terror through the crowd. A great hulk, grayish and shining like leather rose from the opening, and its two large eyes seemed to be fixed upon me. The mouth of the creature was V-shaped with a pointed upper lip. The mouth trembled constantly, and there did not appear to be any chin. It displayed a group of tentacles, and it was evident that the creature's breathing was labored in the foreign atmosphere of earth. A greater gravitational pull than it had known made its movement slow and awkward. It was monstrous and repulsive. Suddenly, it pitched over the mouth of the cylinder and into the pit and was soon followed in the opening by another of these oily brown-skinned creatures. I retreated to a border of trees and looked back to see one of the spectators who had tumbled into the pit struggle up to its edge and then fall back out of sight with a shriek of terror. The crowd had retreated to hedges and gates and whatever would hide them, petrified as they stared at the pit.

CHAPTER 5
The Heat Ray

I had taken cover in the heather and peered out, not knowing just what to expect. However, I did see a long rod rise up from the crater with what seemed to be a wobbling mirror on the top of it. Gradually, knots of people who had scurried when the ugly Martians first emerged from their cylinder began to move back toward the pit. One group in particular, a deputation of sorts, moved ahead waving a white flag in some effort at communicating with the Martians. From the pit came several puffs of greenish smoke and following this a droning noise filled the air, and a humped shape rose up before the onlookers. A bright beam of light sprang out from it and a glaring flame spread over the delegation and those who stood near them. They staggered, fell and were dead, the beam passing over them and igniting brush and trees. The beam of death, a type of heat ray, made a wide sweep incinerating anything in its path. In the distance toward Knaphill, trees and wooden buildings could be seen bursting into flame. Then, as suddenly as it had begun, the droning and hissing that had accompanied the spectacle ceased and the dome-shaped object was withdrawn down into the pit. Only the slender rod with its wobbly mirror on the end remained. At my first opportunity I ran, seized by a terrible and fearful panic. Even with distance, there was no sense of safety, not when that hideous beam could flick on and touch you wherever you were. Later, it became known that Ogilvy, Henderson and the Astronomer Royal, Stent, were in the deputation that had been exterminated by the heat ray.

> **COMMENT:** "Ahead of his time" is a phrase reserved for men with Wells's imaginative and inventive powers. For some reason, it does not do him justice. Such a tale as *The War of*

the Worlds is fresh and stimulating for the reader of today, and yet it was written at the end of the Victorian era when such things as space travel and mysteriously powerful rays belonged to fiction, conceived by the imaginatively impractical of this world. It is evident then that science and civilization have taken better than half a century to overtake Wells, so far had he outdistanced them in his scientific vision. Certainly, space travel is a reality in our own time; and as for the deadly heat ray of the Martians, the great power of modern laser beams is remarkable in its similarity. With Wells, much of the notion of "fiction" must be eliminated in our contemporary use of the term "science fiction."

CHAPTER 6
The Heat Ray in the Chobjam Road

The matter of the Heat Ray is still a mystery to this day. They projected heat and an invisible light, and it may have been that they utilized a type of polished parabolic mirror of some unknown material, using it in a way similar to the manner in which a lighthouse sends out beams. However it worked, it killed forty people during that first confrontation. By eight-thirty, when the deputation had been slain, there may possibly have been three hundred or so of the curious thereabouts. Only a sandy ridge topped with heather saved that crowd of people from being charred out of recognition along with the other forty souls who were unfortunate enough to be caught in the swath of the Heat Ray. This hummock, in fact, had blocked the lower half of the beam and, miraculously, had saved them. The result of the sudden massacre and the blazing trees and bushes was swift panic. People shrieked, some with their clothes aflame, and even a mounted policeman bolted off screaming with his hands clasped to his head. Like startled sheep, they ran; and all the fatalities were not accounted for by the Martians. Two women and a small child were trampled beneath the feet of the hysterical crowd and lay there in darkness and silent terror until death claimed them.

CHAPTER 7
How I Reached Home

I had run wildly and almost insensibly from the site of the massacre until exhaustion brought me to a halt. Incredibly, I was no longer terrified. I had taken hold of myself once again, almost as though the horrors of a short time before had never occurred. My mood was strange; I had experienced it before, a sense of detachment from self and even from the world, of observing from the outside, a watcher removed and untouched by man's tensions and tragedies. This was the way I felt on this night of tragedy.

On the way home, people appeared unaffected by news of events at the common, some of which must have reached them. One woman along the road observed lightly that people had been acting rather silly about the common. Men from Mars, I began, but she laughed, as did the others with her, when I tried to tell what had happened. Once home, I had to take some wine before I could tell my wife what I had seen. She was visibly shaken, but I assured her that the Martian creatures could hardly move and certainly would not be able to get out of the pit. Gravity on earth is three times that of the surface of Mars, and so the Martians' movement here would be incredibly labored. However, what was overlooked on this point was that the earth's atmosphere contains far more oxygen than that of Mars; and this excess would serve as a stimulant to these creatures, counterbalancing, as it were, the leaden quality of their bodies on earth. Overlooked, too, was the fact that their great intelligence would not be that dependent upon muscular exertion.

I recall distinctly the dinner we had on that night. Over wine, I thought of Ogilvy and the impetuous act of the Martians. I felt secure and strengthened by the thought that their slowness of movement reduced the magnitude of their threat considerably. And so it might have been with the extinct dodo bird when some party of hungry sailors landed, complacent and secure that these intruders would be pecked to death on the morrow. How distinctly I see that meal now! I should, for it was the last civilized one I was to have through the nightmarish days that lay ahead.

CHAPTER 8
Friday Night

Outside of a five-mile radius from the sandpit, the news of the Martians was taken quite leisurely. Poor Henderson, who had been in the deputation to the Martians, had sent off a telegram to his London paper about the cylinder; but the wire was not taken seriously when a request for confirmation received no response. Even within the five-mile radius, there was an amazing amount of normal activity considering what had happened. There was some talk, of course, in taverns and from alleged eyewitnesses; but on the whole, things went on as though the Martians had not made their violent descent upon the earth. There were the curious of course, with crowds remaining on the Chobham and Horsell bridges. On the edge of Woking, some half-dozen houses burned as lingering reminders that none of it had been a dream. Some of the bolder spectators had even crawled close to the pit, but these were never seen again. Occasionally, a beam of light would shoot out from the pit; and this preceded the Heat Ray which swept widely about the adjacent area. The common lay bare and deserted through the night and following day, save for the many charred bodies sprawled about. But even from a distance, the sound of hammering could clearly be identified coming from the pit.

That was the situation on Friday night, and as yet no one had the slightest idea of the great conflict that was soon to break out. All through that night, the Martians hammered and lumbered about, preparing the machines they were constructing in the pit, and now and then there arose a puff of greenish smoke. Gradually, the soldiers began to arrive; and it was good to know that the military had some idea of the seriousness of the affair. Shortly after midnight, some people near Woking saw what seemed to be a meteor strike down from the heavens into the pine woods to the northwest. It had a greenish hue and was the second Martian ship to land on earth.

COMMENT: The idea for *The War of the Worlds* sprang from Wells's elder brother, Frank, who shared the author's notion that man was incapable of confronting severe crisis with courage and ability. Thus far in the book, Wells has been careful to emphasize the slack response of those not immediately present at the sandpit massacre. There is a mental unpreparedness evident, an aggravating indifference, and frequent examples of man's woeful characteristic of disbelieving the unprecedented. Even tangibility has not always been convincing, and the immediacy of the Martian disaster is painfully slow in making itself felt among the people.

CHAPTER 9
The Fighting Begins

On Saturday there was a sense of anticipation and suspense in the air to compete with the heat and humidity. The milkman arrived and announced a high-level decision that the Martians were not to be killed if at all possible. A neighbor came by for a chat and remarked with some humor that all this business would really play hob with the insurance companies. After breakfast, I walked to the common and talked with some of the soldiers, who were debating among themselves about the best method of getting at those things in the pit — "Rush 'em," said one — while another was all for shelling them into oblivion. The residents about the perimeter of the common had been evacuated, but on the whole the people felt secure with the military on hand. I returned home for lunch and then acquired an evening paper which announced that new attempts had been made to contact the Martians, but without success. However, the thought of all that military force and armament drawn up about the common granted me the temporary luxury of imagining that the Martians were quite helpless in the bottom of their smoking pit.

As the afternoon progressed, artillery pieces were brought up to shell the second cylinder that had fallen in the pine woods, as well as the one on the common. At about six in the evening, I was at tea with my wife when the sound of a great detonation filled the air. I looked out to see trees in flames, the Oriental College devastated, and the steeple of a small church nearby come crashing to earth. I stood astonished, but soon realized that we were now within range of the Martians' Heat Ray. To remain at the house was out of the question, and we decided to go to my wife's cousin's at Leatherhead. I hastened to the Spotted Dog Inn where I procured a cart and horse from the owner, unconcerned as I was, for the moment, that he might have need of it himself. When I returned to the house, trees were burning nearby. We hastened to load the cart with what valuables we could bring, including the servant's box. A soldier ran by, warning everyone to leave. They're crawling out of the pit, he called — in something like a dish cover. We drove off hurriedly as long fingers of flame rose up into the sky behind us. The air was hot and layers of smoke had spread out far to the east and west. People were running down the road, and I let the horse have his head until we had put the panic and the conflict well behind us. In the air you could hear gunfire, and I concluded that the Martians had set afire everything within range of the Heat Ray.

CHAPTER 10
In the Storm

Leatherhead lies about twelve miles from where we lived in Maybury Hill. We arrived about nine, but I had promised the innkeeper to return his horse and cart and so got started back about eleven o'-clock. Curiously, I felt exhilarated at the idea of returning and perhaps being in on the kill, but my wife was disturbed at my leaving and wept. It was a kind of war fever and it sometimes gets into the blood of civilized people. About midnight I had reached the outskirts of Maybury Hill when a shaft of green fire shot down through the clouds and into a field nearby. It was the third Martian projectile. The horse bolted, and the cart and I were off at a great rate. On the opposite side of Maybury Hill, I spied a large curious object that seemed to be moving down the slope. A storm had gathered, and in the flashing of lightning, I saw the thing distinctly. Incredible! Simply incredible! A massive tripod, taller than several houses and moving with great strides across the landscape. Suddenly, ahead of me, another of these monsters appeared, and my horse seemed to be galloping directly at it. I twisted the horse's head to the right, and in a moment the cart had overturned. The horse was dead, and I was shaken but unhurt, as the lumbering tripod passed by. I could see it closely now. Long tentacles hung from it, and it was surmounted with a hood that moved about like a keenly observant head. In the rear of the main body was what appeared to be a great metallic basket. As it passed by, green smoke ejected from the joints, and it began to emit a strange howling noise. Within moments, it was half a mile off with its companion hovering over what must have been that third Martian cylinder that had shortly before thundered into the nearby field. I decided to make my way to my own house, and on the way made a grim discovery. A body lay along the way. When I turned it over, I discovered the proprietor of the Spotted Dog, the man whose cart I had taken in my haste to escape. Once at my house, I huddled at the foot of the staircase and could not free myself from visions of gleaming monstrosities and the face of the dead innkeeper I had seen on the road.

CHAPTER 11
At the Window

After a while, I went into the living room and drank some whisky against the chill. The storm had passed, and in the sky the illumination from the sandpit was visible and grim outlines of great shapes moved about in the reflection. The entire area in that direction appeared to be on fire. From the window, a wrecked and burning train was visible; elsewhere, except for an occasional running figure, no people could be seen. What terror and devastation must have occurred during those last seven hours! I thought for a while and began to see the relationship between those hulking shapes in the sandpit and the three metallic tripods busily moving about in the flickering glow. A soldier passed the house, cautiously, and I called to him to come on in. He took some whisky to steady his nerves and then told me how he had gone into action about seven in the evening. His horse had thrown him about the moment an artillery piece and its ammunition had blown up behind him. Wiped out, and the smell of charred flesh in the air. Many soldiers had been killed when the monster first rose out of the pit. It had used the Heat Ray and cleared the common of all life. Finally, Woking station and its neighboring houses were incinerated by the thing. Another giant had risen out of the pit; they seemed to have been assembled there. The artilleryman had crawled into a ditch, made his escape, and had gone to Horsell only to find it devastated. He had then made his way toward Maybury with hope of getting on to London. After eating some bread and meat, we ventured upstairs to my study; and as dawn rose, we watched the vast devastation in every direction. Three cowled metallic monsters now stood by the pit; when the day brightened, it appeared that the pit had been enlarged and that the work within it raged as furiously as ever.

CHAPTER 12
What I Saw of the Destruction of Weybridge and Shepperton

As dawn gave way to daylight, the soldier and I withdrew from our observation of the Martians. We decided that the house was unsafe, and the soldier suggested that we gather what food supplies we could. He was to make his way to London to rejoin his battery, while I would go to Leatherhead where my wife waited. As we struck out into the woods, we passed an overturned cart with someone's belongings; in the lane was the body of a man wet through from the overnight hail. We encountered three cavalry soldiers who were rather skeptical of our description of the Martians, but said that it was their duty to ride on and see for themselves. Past Byfleet station we left the pine trees and came out beyond the range of the Heat Ray. Along the road were slow-moving carts containing people and their possessions, and here and there artillery pieces were being set up. At Weybridge, the soldier had hoped to locate headquarters but could not. The town and its roads, thereabouts, were beginning to fill with fugitives and their carts. It should be noted that at one point near Shepperton Lock, where the Wey and Thames meet, there was a ferry. Boats crossed back and forth, and already they were loaded beyond capacity. People still did not understand the magnitude of the situation, believing, as many did, that the Martians were simply formidable humans whose forays would soon be suppressed.

In the direction of Chertsey came the thunder of cannon; the fighting had commenced. No sooner had a passing woman expressed confidence that the military would halt these things than across the fields toward Chertsey four of the gleaming monsters appeared, stretching their way toward the flat meadows. A fifth monster materialized and moved toward us in its characteristic rolling motion. As the crowd stood silent and petrified, the Heat Ray reached out and fired Chertsey. The water, get under the water, I shouted and plunged in myself. The shining giant lumbered forward, and several artillery batteries that had been concealed opened fire. One burst struck the machine flush on the revolving hood, obliterating the Martian that controlled it from within. It staggered, uncontrolled now, and plunged off toward Shepperton, crushing the church there, reeling, toppling, and collapsing into the river in a final spasm of effort. Great erratic puffs of steam arose from the thing and a brown oily liquid jetted up into the air from the joints. Suddenly, the other Martian machines were advancing from Chertsey. The artillery did not halt them, and they moved on to their wrecked comrade, sweeping about with their Heat Rays as they did. The air was choked with smoke, staggering noise and rising steam from the defeated Martian. I stood and watched transfixed, as it were, when suddenly I was aware that the Martians were descending upon me. The Heat Ray swept forward, cremating anyone caught in its path. I was standing in the water at the time, and when the Heat Ray swung past, it turned the river into a boiling cauldron. Foaming super-heated waves were formed and I shrieked in agony as they rolled over me. I recall rather hazily the great foot of a Martian giant nearby, and when I fought my way to shore, I understood that by an incredible stroke of fortune I had survived.

COMMENT: Almost to the moment of conflict, the people do not grasp the great danger that faces them. The soldiers disbelieve, and the citizens think the threats are little more than the acts of some outrageous invaders who will soon be brought to their knees. Everywhere disbelief hangs on, and with it the hard-to-die notion of "it can't happen here."

CHAPTER 13
How I Fell in with the Curate

As it stood, there was nothing between the Martians and London that could stop them, but they appeared to be in no hurry. During the remainder of the afternoon and into the night they seemed to have concentrated on unloading the second and third cylinders that had landed at Addlestone and Pyrford. As for myself, I moved along with the river, since that offered the best protection from the Heat Ray. Along the way, houses were burning and it was curious to see the blazes rage on without the ever-present crowd of the curious. In the late afternoon, I came ashore and lay down to rest. When I awoke I became aware that a curate was seated near me. I asked for water, but he had none. His face betrayed weakness; and when he spoke, his words were concerned only with why such things had happened and what was the nature of man's sins that this catastrophe should befall him. Fire, earthquake, death, he cried, and continued his monologue of pathetic despair. I understood then that events had driven this man's sanity to the very brink. His mind wandered when I spoke, and he was absorbed in melancholy abstractions. I reasoned as best I could with him; and beneath the crescent moon and the still grand sunset, I suggested that we go northward.

CHAPTER 14
In London

My brother had been a medical student in London when the business with the Martians broke out. Saturday's paper in London had carried articles on the planet Mars, but they were general in content and other references were noticeable for their brevity. My brother was not unduly concerned for us, and in general London went about its affairs as usual. Notice was not really taken of events in Woking until Monday, since most Londoners do not read Sunday papers. Londoners are jaded to startling events, and, furthermore, they maintain a deep-seated sense of personal security. Londoners, therefore, had no real conception of what the Martians were like — except for some puffy journalistic references to their sluggishness and creeping awkwardness. Late Sunday afternoon, however, it was learned that the people of Walton and Weybridge and the surrounding area were clogging the roads leading to London. Throughout the day, my brother gathered here and there bits of intelligence about the Martian threat. Gradually, a vague apprehension began to fill the London atmosphere. People returned earlier than usual from their Sunday excursions, but there still endured some wishful thinking about the Martians' inability to get out of the pit. Events of the previous day had not, of course, reached London as yet. Toward sunset a curious brown scum came drifting along the Thames. There was rumor concerning a floating body, and someone told my brother about a heliograph signaling in the west. He was quick to get hold of a special edition newspaper that was just out and became aware at last of the incredible circumstances that had occurred. He learned also that the Martians were not invulnerable, that it was hoped that any additional cylinders could be destroyed before they became a greater threat. The news finally got to the people and converted their apathy to concern and agitation. Going toward Trafalgar Square, my brother spied some of the refugees from West Surrey with a cart and some belongings. Other carts came by, and the occupants gave out the news to people as they passed. The Martians, they cried, like boilers on stilts, walking like men, too. In the south of London, one could distinctly hear the sounds of artillery, and the refugees continued to steam in. My brother read and reread the papers, and it was not until after midnight that he went to bed. In the ordinarily peaceful hours of the morning, he was awakened by commotion in the streets, a pounding on doors, a routing out of people with the news that the Martians had broken through defenses and that London was in danger. It was the beginning of a great panic. In the streets people were running about frantically. A newspaper vendor, now selling his papers for little or nothing, raced past. My brother got hold of one and learned that the Martians were now shooting out vast clouds of black smoke, a dense poisonous vapor that smothered the artillery batteries. They were moving toward London, and it was impossible to halt them. People now scurried from buildings and out into the streets. Church bells struck out a chorus of alarm. My brother then got together the ten pounds or so he had on hand and went back out into the streets.

> **COMMENT:** Complacency has now given way to terror and panic in London, and a great outpouring of refugees from London has begun. However, there is a new development. The Martians are using a thick poisonous cloud that settles over the gun batteries and suffocates the men. Here, couched in the science fiction of Wells's fertile imagination, is the essence of gas warfare, soon to be a standard tactic in the great conflict of World War I which lay only sixteen years ahead of the publication of *The War of the Worlds* in 1898.

CHAPTER 15
What Happened in Surrey

About eight o'clock in the evening of the day I had met the curate, three of the Martian machines came out from the pit at Horsell where the Martians had been working feverishly. They moved toward Weybridge and Ripley and had the good fortune to face inexperienced gunners who bolted and ran at the first encounter. At St. George's Hill, the affair was different. The men held their ground, fired a good volley, struck one of the Martians squarely, and down he went. The fallen Martian sent out long variable howls of the same nature that these creatures used to communicate with one another. When the other two Martians were alerted, they sent out their Heat Rays, and the gun batteries were silenced. The Martians repaired their damaged machine and were soon joined by four of their fellows. It was then about nine at night. They distributed thick black tubes among themselves, spread out in a line, and advanced.

The curate and I were hurrying along a road that runs out of Halliford, and we spied more of these huge machines, as well as warning rockets that shot up from the hills as soon as the monsters were in motion. The curate panicked at the sight of the Martians and began to run, but he changed his mind and joined me when he saw that I had taken cover. The Martians took up position in a wide crescent, a type of battle formation, but their occasional howling communication to one another had given way to total silence. They now faced Staines, Hounslow, Ditton, Esher and Ockham—and waiting for them were the guns. There was, indeed, that inflammable silence before battle, a high pitch of anticipation, terrifying and thrilling simultaneously. I wondered then, as so many others must have, how well the Martians understood the people on earth. I wondered if they were aware that we were organized, that we were disciplined beings, or did they believe we could be scattered at will. I thought then of London. Would there be pitfalls to trap the Martians? Would the Londoners make a stand? Had they the courage and doggedness to make their defense a sublime Moscow?

As the Martians moved forward, the curate and I watched and were puzzled by the fact that the artillery made no response to the Martian movement. The aluminum giants were firing out canisters from the tubes they carried. These canisters had come to earth and spread out a thick black vapor, pouring out in all directions in a gaseous cloud, suffocating anything in its path. It clung in dense cloud banks, and only after some time would it sink to earth as a dust. To this day we do not really understand its composition. The Martians also had complete control of this gas once it was dispersed. If they wished, they could direct a force of steam against it and it would dissipate. It was about this time, moreover, that the fourth Martian cylinder struck the earth, somewhere near Bushey Park. The Martians were now laying down their deadly gas toward London, and by midnight the whole of the Thames valley had been blotted out by thick black smoke. After Sunday night, there was no organized opposition to these creatures. Even the gunboats and destroyers would not stand fast as the crews mutinied, rendering the boats useless. By daybreak the poisonous vapor had engulfed Richmond, and the government was emphasizing vigorously the need for flight.

CHAPTER 16
The Exodus from London

Thus, by Monday a great surge of fear had swept through the city. By midday police and government in general seemed to be melting into a state of inoperation. Trains were mobbed and, once at their destinations, did not return, for the crews refused to bring them back to London. The roads were not yet glutted, and my brother having taken to the avenues leaving London acquired a bicycle in the looting of a cycle shop. At about seven he reached Edgeware, where he acquired some food at the inn. My brother had thought perhaps of making his way to Chelmsford where some friends resided, and so he struck out on a lonely lane that ran eastward. He encountered few people along the way until he happened upon two ladies in a small carriage who were struggling with three assailants. My brother rushed to the situation and engaged the men, knocking one to the ground. He grabbed a second robber and was struck in the face by a third. In the ensuing battle the small carriage with the two women in it raced off, with my brother and two of his adversaries in pursuit. It would not have gone well for him had not the younger and more slender of the two women brought the vehicle about, returned and fired a shot from a revolver at my brother's antagonists. In no time the attackers had gotten their fill and made off down the road and out of sight.

Thus, my brother found himself somewhat battered about the face and hands, and riding off on an unfamiliar road with these two women. It seems they were the wife and younger sister of a surgeon who had learned of the Martian invasion and sent them on ahead with provisions and a revolver. He was to overtake them but had not appeared. My brother promised to remain with them. Over the frantic objections of Mrs. Elphinstone, the surgeon's wife, it was decided to strike out across Essex toward Harwich in an effort to leave the country. The slender woman, the surgeon's younger sister, was remarkably composed and made a sharp contrast to her sister-in-law's unreasonableness. As they drove on in the chaise, they encountered more and more people, some wild-eyed and haggard, others disheveled and unclean. The traffic increased until they came upon the crossroads and an unbelievable throng of humanity, tumbling and pressing close upon one another in a great torrent of dust and vehicles and feverish voices. Carts and carriages blundered together, overburdened with the old and young. Voices and sounds of every description filled the air. Oaths and prayers, stern commands and distraught weeping all combined in one inarticulate cry of humanity on the move. My brother and his companions halted and considered this impossible current of frantic human beings. A coach pulled up and the driver asked for water. His passenger was the Lord Garrick, the Chief Justice, and he was dying. My brother went to the assistance of a poor wretch who had tumbled down before the oncoming crowds. A bundle of coins the man carried scattered out. He shrieked and defied rescue, and so was trampled under hoof and wagon wheel. My brother and the two ladies turned back from the main road; it was a nightmare. However, after a moment of deliberation he advised Miss Elphinstone that, horrible as it was, the main road must be taken. The young lady proved herself once again, and with some hazardous effort, they forced the chaise into the streaming throng and were swept along without a will of their own. Further on the road forked, and they were able to strike out towards Hadley. Later in the afternoon they managed to halt by the side of the road, exhausted, hungry, and afraid to sleep.

COMMENT: The great throng of humanity on the road is a mixture of all walks and degrees of life. The lowest level of society jostles with the coach of the Chief Justice for room to escape. This chapter must make the reader acutely aware of Wells's magnificent descriptive powers. Henry James likened them to those of Dickens and the comparison does honor to both novelists. One need only refer to the mob scenes in Dickens' *A Tale of Two Cities* to discover the artistic alertness to sight and sound that both men share. Both Dickens and Wells appear most able in their sweeping portrayals of thundering, uncontrolled humanity, insensate and blind to reason or mercy. Both are able to capture the repulsive excitement generated by the fierceness of irrational mobs, and so create notably powerful word pictures, vigorously done and not soon forgotten when the page is turned.

CHAPTER 17
The "Thunder Child"

The rout of humanity was more than that; it was a stampede that promised the massacre of mankind. The Martians were calm and methodical about everything, spreading out the cloud of death at will and clearing it away with steam jets. Certainly, many Londoners remained in the city through Monday, and it is equally certain that a great number were suffocated there by the Black Smoke. The harbor at London had its incredible aspect as well. Many people had swum out to the boats at anchor, some attempting bribery, others simply pleading to be taken on—and many, it seems, were driven off with boat hooks and drowned. About one in the afternoon, some of the Black Cloud appeared near Blackfriars Bridge and prompted a great press of vessels in the northern arch of the Tower Bridge. About two o'clock a Martian appeared, but by then both people and boats had fled.

The fifth and sixth Martian cylinders then fell to earth, and my brother had seen the latter tumble out of the heavens in the distance towards Wimbledon. As my brother and his companions drove on, it became more evident that the general shortage of food had become acute. Private property ceased to be respected and farmers had to defend their crops and cattle with arms. On Wednesday my brother and his two lady companions were unfortunate enough to encounter a self-styled Committee of Public Supply which seized their pony as a contribution to a communal food supply.

When ships were no longer able to come up the Thames, they had to make their way to the Essex coast, to Harwich and Walton, and to other locations where they might take in refugees. There were vessels of all flags and descriptions—English, Scotch, French, Dutch, Swedish—and everything from trim liners to a whole host of filthy colliers. Stretched out in a long thin line down the Channel were the ironclads, the nearest one being the torpedo-ram *Thunder Child*. It was with some difficulty that my brother and Miss Elphinstone got her panicky sister-in-law aboard a channel steamer, so unwilling was she to leave England. At last a bargain was struck—thirty-six pounds for the three of them—and after the vessel was loaded beyond capacity, it finally got under way.

The ship was making her way eastward when one, two, and then three Martians appeared in the distance, making their way directly toward the shipping on the coast. As the Martians advanced out into the water, my brother watched fascinated rather than afraid, and along with the other spectators was cheered heartily as the ironclad *Thunder Child* swung past and made for the Martians. A canister of the Black Cloud was shot at the ironclad but bounced off her armor harmlessly. One of the Martians discharged the Heat Ray, striking the oncoming ship, but it was too late; the monster was struck soundly, reeled and pitched headlong into the sea. The *Thunder Child* had been damaged but the Martian was down, steaming and sputtering in the waters of the Channel. The ironclad then headed for the second Martian and was within a hundred yards when the Heat Ray struck. The vessel shuddered with internal explosions but kept her heading. Riding on momentum alone, she struck the underpinnings of the aluminum hulk, crippled it and sent it tumbling down to destruction in a froth of steaming water. By this time, the other ironclads were moving in toward shore, and the steamer had put good distance between itself and the third Martian, now disappearing in the mists and steam. Quite soon the sun began to slide into the gray clouds on the horizon, and the steamer captain suddenly directed everyone's attention toward the distance. Something had rushed out of the grayness in the western heavens, something that appeared flat and broad and rather large. The thing swung across the sky quickly in an arch and just as suddenly dropped off into the grayness from which it arose.

COMMENT: The Martians are not invincible and an ironclad, an early armored warship, has brought two of them down. On the horizon a strange flat and broad object streaks across the sky, and Wells's description makes us think of modern-day reports of unidentified flying objects. Later in the book it will be mentioned that the Martians may have been experimenting with flight on earth—this sighting may have been one of those experimental ships.

BOOK II
CHAPTER 1
Underfoot

While my brother made his way to the coast and had finally gotten off across the Channel, the curate and I had secreted ourselves in a deserted house in Halliford where we had fled from the Black Smoke. I was concerned about my wife and the fact that she must surely have given up hope, but I was constantly returned to the immediacy of our situation by the woeful ejaculations and selfish despair of the curate. The Black Smoke had drifted our way, and for a time we were trapped. However, a Martian had come by and dispersed the vile fumes with a jet of steam. Thus, a way was laid open to escape. The curate was afraid to leave and his presence had come to pall upon me heavily; I resolved then to leave him—and should have immediately. I gathered what supplies I could, and it was only when the curate was convinced that I would leave him that he finally joined me in quitting the abandoned house. About five in the afternoon, we took to the road leading to Sunbury. On our way it was impossible to avoid grotesquely sprawled human bodies, as well as those of horses near their overturned carts. For the most part, they were covered with the settled dust of the Black Smoke and urgently reminded me of what I had read of the destruction of Pompeii.

We crossed the Richmond Bridge, and I was struck by the presence of curious red masses floating down the river—as it turned out I credited them with being more dire than they were. We approached Kew, and suddenly a Martian towered above us. We hid in a garden shed, and all the while the curate trembled and muttered to himself. We pushed on again when it seemed safe to do so. Then, across a field was another Martian; but this time rather than killing the frantic figures that scurried about beneath him, he was plucking them up and depositing them in the strange metallic cage that he wore behind him. Obviously, the Martians had some particular plan in mind for defeated humanity. We crouched in a ditch then and did not emerge until eleven o'clock at night. Along the way, we happened upon a fine white house with a walled garden. There we discovered half a ham, some bread and an uncooked steak. There was lettuce, too, and even some bottled beer. The curate was agitated and all for pressing on, but I insisted we remain and eat what we could to bolster our strength.

It was nearly midnight when a brilliant green light flared outside the house. It was followed closely by a massive concussion that seemed to smash everything breakable in the house and hurled me across the room and into unconsciousness. When I revived the curate was wiping my forehead with water and advising me not to move — *they* were out there. From the outside came the distinct sound of a metallic rattle; but we only listened to it, wisely refraining from moving for some three or four hours. A great mass of garden earth had been heaped up against the window. Through it we could make out a twisted drainpipe against the house. With the light of dawn, we saw it — the fifth cylinder with a Martian standing watch over it; the enormous concussion was the result of its arrival. For a long time we waited in silence, and then I crawled about searching for food. The curate, who had been whimpering revoltingly, did not accompany me when I slithered off; but once I was gone he was quick to catch up.

CHAPTER 2
What I Saw from the Ruined House

We could hear various machine noises coming from outside the house, and after some cautious maneuvering, we gained a vantage point to survey just exactly what was going on out there. The house had almost been completely crushed by the Martian cylinder when it landed. The Martians were now working in a great pit with the cylinder already opened. I was struck immediately by an extremely intricate and active machine which was busily at work. It was so agile, with a living quality about it, reminding one of a metallic spider with tentacles around its body. It was really what we call a handling machine. For the first time I was able to make a really careful study of the Martians' appearance. They were the most revolting and unearthly beings imaginable. Their large round bodies were actually heads, and each had a face in the front, two large eyes and a surface in the rear of the head which acted as an ear. About the beaklike mouth were sixteen tentacles that were used as hands. Subsequent dissection of a Martian revealed an amazingly simple internal anatomy. He was mostly brain, and the remainder of his organs consisted of two large lungs, a heart and its vessels. It should be noted as well that the Martians did not eat food but rather lived on warm blood, which in most instances they obtained from still living people. This, no doubt, is horrible to consider, but our own carnivorous habits might appear equally as revolting to some gentle animal suddenly made intelligent.

Furthermore, the Martians did not sleep, since they had no complicated muscular system to become fatigued. These creatures were sexless also, and so were free of the profound emotionalism associated with that human characteristic. Their young, and there was a Martian born on earth during invasion, were attached to the parent and simply budded off when they reached a certain size. In our own order of things, such a method of propagation has disappeared. It was at best a primitive method and co-existed with the bi-sexual methods even up to the first cousins of vertebrate creatures, and in time the sexual procedure predominated. On Mars then the process had reversed itself.

I recall having seen once a facetious article suggesting that ultimately the perfection of mechanical devices would supersede the human limbs in efficiency. All superfluous organs then, said the writer, would diminish and only the brain and the hand would survive. Written facetiously, to be sure, but with the Martians the intelligent and manual had taken precedence over the purely animal in their natures. In addition, the Martians differed from man in that they had eliminated micro-organisms from their planet. Germs, therefore, were unknown to them, along with the myriad diseases and disorders known to human life.

Another oddity concerning the Martians was the presence of their red weed. By the third or fourth day that the curate and I were hidden in the house, this red vegetation had grown up out of the pit. Its growth was exceptionally vigorous, and later I discovered that it had proliferated throughout the countryside, most abundantly wherever there was water.

Communication between the Martians was an extraordinary thing. There was a monotone hooting that preceded feeding, but this appeared only to have been part of a physical preparation for the ingestion of human blood described before. Thus, I am certain that they communicated by a manner of thought exchange without any gesture or vocal agency whatsoever. The Martians had evolved into a thoroughly cerebral state. They were simply brains with the ability to transfer themselves to various mechanical "bodies" according to the task to be performed. The discovery of the wheel had either eluded them, incredibly, or else they had advanced beyond its practical use, for their machinery did not seem to require its function.

I crouched in my hiding place and closely watched the handling machine. It seemed even more alive than the Martians themselves with their cumbersome gravity-impeded motion. The machine worked diligently and could be observed selecting parts and assembling a mechanism in its own image.

COMMENT: This chapter should be read and reread, for it contains so much of Wells's science fiction that has now ceased to be fiction. The handling machines strike the reader with their robotlike characteristics, and bear a similarity to the type of remote-controlled mechanism that our own space scientists are preparing for work on other planets. Wells's passing reference to a humorous article suggesting that mechanical devices must someday take the place of human limbs goes to the heart of automation in which mechanical proficiency outstrips human manual efforts, and fewer and fewer men are required for a particular manufacturing task. The narrator has remarked on the Martians' ability to communicate by thought transmission rather than by speech. Here, certainly, is the concept of telepathic communication so hotly debated today. Wells sees the Martians as an extremely advanced stage of evolution, a point at which the dependence upon mind *and* body had shifted overwhelmingly in favor of intelligence. Their own bodies have mutated with superfluous organs dwindling to nonexistence; they have been reduced to the simplest organ systems, highly developed intelligences far beyond man's humble capacities.

In reading this chapter the reader should become acutely aware of the reasonableness of Wells's descriptions and explanations of the Martians. Nowhere does he seem to defy probability or plausibility. What he says is reasonable, and the abilities of the Martians impress us as the inevitable result of a natural process that for man is only in its elementary stages. Today, of course, Wells's arguments have even more validity, for many of the incredible devices and propositions he advances here have become or are about to become all too real. Interplanetary travel, the basic ability necessary for *The War of the Worlds* is about to be realized in our time. Wells's fantasies are, to be sure, terrifyingly prophetic in many ways. He was a visionary, but any appraisal of him as an impractical fictionalizer is woefully inaccurate in the light of contemporary scientific achievements.

CHAPTER 3
The Days of Imprisonment

A second Martian giant arrived, which made us even more cautious in peeping at the busy activity in the pit. Unfortunately, the curate and I were totally incompatible; there were often fierce struggles to get to an opening and observe the invaders. The curate had a blind stubbornness to him and was a constant annoyance with his habit of muttering pitifully and helplessly. He wept, he had no self-control, he slept little and ate and drank frantically. However, he was cunning and shifty in adversity and was an immediate threat to our security in the ruined house. He was one of those beings who faced neither man, nor Creator, nor even himself. In the secret darkness of our imprisonment, we clawed and kicked one another between violent whispers, while outside the Martians proceeded in a determined way with their orderly activity. On one occasion the curate came sliding down the rubbish heap from the point from which we watched, clutching his head, pointing to the opening, but incapable of communicating articulately. I scrambled up and beheld to my horror that the Martians had a human being, one that had probably been plucked up and kept in the cage each carried behind. It was evident that they were now draining his blood for nourishment. The sight of this had sent the curate over the brink of irrationality. I fought to maintain my own self-control and was successful in this, but the curate had already degenerated to a level barely above the response of an animal. I had contemplated escaping by excavation, but I could not depend upon the curate, and the pathetic effort I made at digging proved futile—and so I gave up the idea completely. On the evening of the third day, we were still imprisoned in the collapsed house. Gazing at the serene beauty of the fading heavens, I heard the sound of great guns firing. Six times they sounded, and then six times again—and then there was silence.

> **COMMENT:** It is interesting here to contrast the measured efficiency of the Martians and their machines with the futile situation of the two human beings in the demolished house. The irrational, muddled responses of the curate provide a particularly strong contrast. His education and the philosophical and theological support that his vocation should provide him, dissolve in the face of these extraordinary horrors. His mind is gone and the animal in him has superseded the intellectual, the reverse of what has evolved for the Martians.

CHAPTER 4
The Death of the Curate

On the sixth day I discovered the curate back in the scullery drinking wildly from a bottle of burgundy. I told him we would begin a discipline about the food and drink, but he would observe none of it; by the eighth day, he would no longer whisper and refused to moderate his voice in any way. It was obvious; he was insane. His mind wandered from mumblings about God's just punishment on man to a sudden consideration of the food; this would be accompanied by pleading, weeping, and always concluded with threats. This continued through the eighth and ninth days. Then he would be still no longer and rose and boomed out that the word of the Lord was upon him, and he would bear witness. In a moment he was running in an effort to escape. I snatched up a meat cleaver and was after him. Fear of discovery overcame me, and I struck him in the head with the butt edge of the instrument. Almost immediately, one of the handling machines appeared in a smashed opening in the wall. I saw clearly the hideous face of the Martian operating it—probing, probing with its long tentacles. Petrified, I withdrew into the coal cellar and could hear the creature examining the body of the curate. I could hear something at the door latch and then a long affair like an elephant's trunk was thrust in, exploring and carefully feeling its way over the contents of the room. It scratched and tapped along the walls, moving slowly and methodically as it went. Once the thing even touched my boot, and I nearly cried out in terror. At last it was satisfied and withdrew. Throughout the tenth day I lay there, and not until the eleventh day did I chance any movement from the coals and firewood and crawl out for the drink I so desperately needed.

CHAPTER 5
The Stillness

To my despair I discovered that the Martian had made off with every bit of food that had been in the pantry. On the eleventh and twelfth days, I had no food or drink. I gambled then and managed some impure rain water from a creaking pump near the sink. On the thirteenth day I drank more of the tainted water and dozed, but my thoughts and dreams were disturbed by visions of the curate. On the fourteenth day, I realized that the red weed which had come up out of the pit now covered the large hole in the wall. On the fifteenth day, a dog peered in at me and began to bark. I tried to lure him in with the idea of killing him for safety's sake, as well as providing myself with something to eat. I listened, but the pit was silent. I made my way to the peephole and saw that the pit was now empty save for some birds that picked at the skeletons of the people consumed by the Martians. Happily, no Martians were visible anywhere. I emerged and I stood in the brilliant glow of the day. Everywhere the red weed had spread out, completely covering the open ground. I breathed deeply, and it was good to savor the sweetness of the air.

CHAPTER 6
The Work of Fifteen Days

I was thoroughly startled by this bizarre carpet of red weed that confronted me after fifteen days of imprisonment. I felt alone, no longer master of my world, but tentative and weak under Martian domination. I felt that man had been dethroned. The red weed was everywhere, and sometimes I was neck deep as I moved along. It crept over everything in its path, and its huge water fronds had even choked the Wey and the Thames rivers. Eventually, this red growth died off almost as rapidly as it had grown, the fronds bleaching and shriveling as the result of earthly bacteria upon them. Bacteria had been eliminated on Mars but not on earth where vegetation has developed certain powers of resistance. As I walked on toward Putney, no human beings were to be seen, and besides a few onions and gladiola bulbs, the only other food I could locate was some crushed bones of rabbits and sheep — and these I gnawed avidly. As I made my way along the road, I was greatly depressed by the suspicion that man had now been exterminated and only a few survivors such as myself remained. They may be done with England already, I thought, and may now be ravaging Paris or Berlin or the European cities to the north.

CHAPTER 7
The Man on Putney Hill

That night was passed in the inn located atop Putney Hill. I found some pitiful half-rotted scraps of food and two tins of pineapple. My mind, however, was preoccupied by three considerations: the killing of the curate, the Martians and just where they might be now, and what had become of my wife. As for the death of the curate, I experienced no remorse. Events had led almost inevitably toward it from the moment we had begun traveling together. He could not cooperate, and I could see how I had been drawn inexorably to that fatal blow. Yet, the memory of the act remained, and in the quiet of the night, conscious of God's presence, I felt myself on trial for that sudden moment of violence. I thought of my wife then, and I prayed that if she had been struck down by the Heat Ray that it had been merciful in its swiftness. I had not prayed since the night of my return from Leatherhead and my wife. Now I prayed, not by rote, mouthing words like mysterious charms, but with awareness and sobriety, face to face with my Creator here in the darkness surrounded by a mutilated countryside. I crept out of the inn, conscious of having spoken with God but insignificant and inferior in a land now dominated by superior beings. If this terrible scourge has drawn a single forceful lesson for humanity, it is one that counsels us to greater compassion for whatever wretched souls are subject to our own authority.

It was June, and the morning was a rich pink in the eastward sky with occasional touches of golden clouds here and there. As I paused contemplating my loneliness and the desire to reach Leatherhead, I suddenly found myself facing a ragged man with a cutlass, claiming the area as his own and demanding to know where I was going. In a moment we had recognized each other. It was the soldier, the artilleryman, I now faced. We greeted each other warmly and I discovered from him that, from what he had observed, the Martians had constructed a flying machine and were learning to fly. At this news I conceded that it was all over for humanity. But this artilleryman had formulated magnificent plans for survival. The sturdiest of men and women, people made for survival, would go underground—the sewers under London would be best. The best books of science must be gotten from the libraries and museums so that our learning would be preserved. There would always be those pitiful humans that would go like lambs to their captivity. For them it was just as well, but not for us, said the artilleryman. We must live on, and live on independently, he cried. I was astounded by his courage and range of thought, a common soldier. But I was soon to realize he was little more than an enthusiastic dreamer. Kept alive by his hopes and grandiose plans for capturing a Martian machine, he was more than willing to put off diligent effort until a later time, giddy with the notion that it would be he who would drive the captured machine wildly about the countryside. He was more interested in dreaming, drinking and gluttony of the food he had stored there, and as he said—one can always work. I was greatly disillusioned, and I resolved to leave him and to press on toward London.

COMMENT: It is interesting at this point to contrast the two types of individuals the narrator has encountered. The curate, for all his faith, was a weak man, the kind the artilleryman spoke of with contempt when he said that there would always be those pious, will-of-God people, all psalms and do-nothing religion. The curate's inability to cope with violent realities contrasts sharply with the artilleryman's seemingly well-ordered planning about survival, survival with dignity and hope. However, despite the wide disparity in their natures, one is as ineffectual as the other. The curate merely shrivels into insanity and religious terror, while the ineffectual soldier revels in a froth of noble dreams and pitifully self-heroic visions.

CHAPTER 8
Dead London

When I left the artilleryman, I went in the direction of Pulham. The red weed which had been so abundant everywhere was now withering rapidly from the spreading disease that had settled upon it. The heavy dust of the Black Smoke was everywhere. I came upon a man rolling about on the ground, deliriously drunk and black with dust. I would have stayed to assist him, but he became so brutally violent that I thought better of it. Toward Brompton, the dead became more abundant, grotesquely postured beside the road, some having been dead long enough to be offensive. When I was well into London I became intensely aware of the profound silence. It was near South Kensington that I first heard the eerie howling, a mournful two-note wailing that eventually I placed in the area of Regent's Park. The sound played upon my mind and nerves and my spirits sank noticeably. What was I doing in this desolate city? Was I alone? I despaired. I thought of the dead and the maniacal drunk I had seen, and my mind turned to old friends, to wines — and to poisons. I then broke into a public house and was fortunate to find food and drink. By this time it was dusk, and I followed a course in the direction of Baker Street. It was there that I caught sight of the howling Martian in the distance. I experienced no fear but simply stood there and watched. It was extraordinary, for the great machine was motionless and crying out hauntingly in that same two-note wail. I then encountered a wrecked handling machine that looked as if it had run wildly into a building and been smashed. Darkness was coming on and prevented me from spying the dead Martian that lay there, rent to pieces by dogs that had come upon his corpse. Then, all at once the terrible wail from the distant Martian giant ceased, and the silence that fell upon the city was suffocating. I despaired totally. It was unendurable, and I could go no further. I turned, ran, and hid myself in a cab driver's shelter until after midnight.

By dawn my courage had returned, but I was possessed by a firm resolve to let myself die. I marched resolutely towards a Martian I saw on Primrose Hill. It would not be necessary to kill myself; it would be done for me. Suddenly, I was stunned. About the hood of the machine where the Martian sat were a group of circling birds. I ran wildly and with amazing energy to where the grim giant stood impotent. From out of the hood hung shreds of a brown substance, evidence of the fury with which the birds had clawed and torn at this dead creature from another planet. I came upon other Martian machines, and each was the same — silent and motionless, with its occupant dead. The Martians were dead, slain by infectious bacteria against which they were defenseless on earth. The humblest creations in God's universe had brought about the Martians' destruction. Germs had taken their enormous toll on man in the past, and with this price man had purchased certain bacterial immunities. But more important than this, he had maintained his birthright to a planet the Martians had futilely sought to wrest from him. As I looked about me at this London, this great city in ruins and with it the efforts and hopes of millions, I realized also that the pall had been lifted and that this dead city would once again rise in greatness. My emotion was almost unbearable. I thought of my wife then and of the life we had known, ended now forever.

COMMENT: The gradual deterioration of the once vibrant red weed is a foreshadowing of the eventual demise of the Martians themselves — and both perish through the same affliction — disease bacteria to which they are woefully susceptible. It is ironic, indeed, for such highly sophisticated beings to have been brought down by microscopic creatures invisible to the naked eye. There is an overall lesson in humility and hope in this chapter. All of man's weaponry failed to halt the Martians, and man could in no way claim a portion of that victory. All that remains to man is his resurgent spirit and a strength born of humility.

CHAPTER 9
Wreckage

It is a strange fact that I know nothing of the three days that followed my discovery of the Martian dead. I had not been the first to discover them, for others had managed to telegraph Paris and thus to spread the wonderful news throughout the world. People had poured back into London. Church bells peeling, people crying out in deliverance, ships converging on the city in great numbers — all this was unknown to me for three days as I wandered dazed and unresponsive to what was going on about me. I had been sheltered by some benevolent people. When I had regained my senses, I was told that every soul in Leatherhead had been destroyed. My friends tried to dissuade me from leaving them, but my mind was made up, and I began my journey back to Woking and the little house in which my wife and I had lived. On my way out of London, I purchased a copy of a flimsy sheet that was the first effort at republishing newspapers. Close examination of the Martians and their mechanisms had revealed many marvels, among which, the paper claimed, was the fact that they had mastered the secret of flying. At Waterloo Station, I boarded a train and was shortly on my way to Woking. The line to Woking had not been completely repaired, and so I took to the road for the remainder of the distance. When I passed a smashed cart and the shattered bones of a horse, my memory was immediately jolted. When I reached my house, it was much as I had left it four weeks before. In my study were some of the sheets I had been working on, treating of moral ideas and the civilizing process. I gazed about. The house was deserted; only ghosts remained here. Then I heard voices behind me. I turned and hurried to the French windows to behold my wife and cousin. "You came," she cried, "I knew, I knew. . . ."

CHAPTER 10
The Epilogue

I am a speculative philosopher, and so I regret that I cannot add substantively to the discussion of the many problems concerning the Martians, problems as yet unsolved. However, an examination of the dead Martians did reveal that no bacteria other than what was known on earth was discovered on them. They seem to have made no effort to bury their dead; and, of course, this fact, plus the irresponsible manner in which they slaughtered humans and left them to rot would tend to indicate that they had no idea of putrefaction and its results. As for the Black Smoke and the generator for the Heat Rays, they remain in the province of unsolved mystery. I am conscious, however, of the need for humanity to be on guard against additional attacks from the Martians. It is certainly not beyond possibility, and yet they have lost such a tremendous advantage in the failure of their first assault. Nevertheless, the attack has caused humanity to regard the future in fresh perspective. We can no longer regard earth as man's inviolable territory, immune to whatever beneficial or malign forces may arrive from the universe. Our complacent surety about the future has been corrected considerably, and there has developed a keen concern for the well-being of man. We have been persuaded also of the existence of life on planets other than our own. And just as the Martians were able to journey to earth, so when our planet becomes uninhabitable through the cooling of the sun, then it may be that man will himself reach out into the universe and travel to a more habitable sphere in the heavens. My vision of man's future in the vastness of space is marvelous, indeed, but it may be that it is the Martians and not humanity who shall be the inheritors of that future. Time and time again the grotesque vision of those four weeks work their way through my memory in all too vivid a fashion, grim and strange—but the strangest experience of all is to hold my wife's hand tenderly in my own and to think that there was a time when we reckoned each other among the numberless dead.

CHARACTER ANALYSIS

In *The War of the Worlds* there is really but one central character — the narrator. The remaining characters worth examining are his brother, the curate, the artilleryman, Miss Elphinstone, and even Mrs. Elphinstone. The curate and the artilleryman appear to be extreme opposites in their responses to the catastrophe of the Martian invasion. The curate gives way to fear, impotence and finally insanity. His answer to calamity is not to struggle courageously but to assign the situation to the will of God, punishing men for their sins. Religious orthodoxy and formality are handled roughly by Wells in his books, and the curate in *The War of the Worlds* suggests the breakdown of rote spiritualism in the face of unaccountable and formidable crisis.

The artilleryman seems capable of confronting the Martian problem with greater than average strength and resourcefulness. He appears capable and ingenious in the face of a bleak future for man. He impresses us with his unwillingness to be a lamb to the slaughter but will draw upon cunning and foresight to preserve scientific knowledge against a time of triumph over the invaders. But soon enough, the narrator sees that the artilleryman's spirited fiber is a flimsy construction at best. He abounds with plans, with unquenchable hope for man, with ingenious schemes for man's survival — but he will begin work on them another day. There is always time for work, but now is the time for eating, for drinking and for dreaming of heroic encounters with the Martians. The artilleryman is disappointingly transparent. His unconquerable spirit reveals itself as a tissue of self-glorifying illusion. He is only a man of words, never actions. In reality then the curate and the artilleryman, apparently poles apart, meet eventually in a common bond of frailty and human insufficiency.

But what of the narrator? The narrator of course is the voice of Wells and, like the central characters in the other books examined in this guide, is a projection of Wells himself. The narrator is self-sufficient and capable, but Wells wisely permits him a proper portion of human weakness. He is at times thoroughly frightened, yet never panicky, and near the end of the book manifests a moment of understandable despair, prompted more by exhaustion, it seems, than by character weakness. He has a humility that is becoming but never snivels before the Martian dangers. The narrator's brother is of course a second self or projection of the narrator, and so of Wells too. He acts prudently, courageously, and maintains a dignified self-composure that avoids the extremes of terrified resignation, crowd panic or simpering defeat. His female partner in the pursuit of dignified human survival is Miss Elphinstone, who shares his composure and strength, a young woman whose qualities are clearly contrasted by the incapacities of her sister-in-law Mrs. Elphinstone. Mrs. Elphinstone cannot lead; she must be controlled and directed in crisis. She is to some degree a companion figure for the scattered, disoriented character of the curate, and represents additional strength for Wells's belief in humanity's insufficiency, a social softness bred by the corruption of complacency and self-satisfaction.

TONO-BUNGAY
BOOK THE FIRST
The Days Before Tono-Bungay Was Invented

CHAPTER I
Of Bladesover House, and My Mother; and the Constitution of Society

The course of most people's lives seems to follow a pattern of beginning, middle and end, and they are not usually out of character. A person usually has his class and remains there during the course of his life. There are others, however, who encounter life on different levels, tasting, as it were, the various strata. Sometimes one is extracted from one's class, out of one's stratum, and lives rather crosswise for the rest of one's days. This has been my lot in life, and I have received many impressions from it. I want, therefore, to tell about it, and that is why I have attempted a novel. I have known a countess, been married and divorced by the daughter of a gasworks clerk, and tumbled champagne on the trousers of a splendid statesman of the empire. Moreover, I have even murdered a man. Yes, I have been in contact with a great variety of people, but extensive relationships with the extremes of the social orders — royalty and the laboring classes — have been limited, indeed. However, my remarkable social range of experience is simply part of the accident of birth, as is so much in England. But I was the nephew of Edward Ponderevo, that Napoleon of enterprise who with his Tono-Bungay [patent medicine] streaked across the financial heavens like a comet. I was his nephew and his close associate, and I clung to his coattails through the whole affair.

You should know at the outset that this book will be something of a mixture. I wish to trace the path that my uncle and I took, but I must advise you that my ideas of writing a novel do not fall into very rigid or formal patterns. Tono-Bungay can still be seen on the market, and even though its financial aura has faded, it still quiets the cough and brightens the elderly eye. And I am the only survivor of the affair, sitting here with my scientific work in a world far removed from that of Tono-Bungay. What I really want to tell about is myself, and of the opinions I have formed about what we call society, and the ways we are driven and lured into its dire intricacies. Thus I am writing my one novel, and avoiding the accepted rules of construction, since I have found them impossible for me. Certainly, it is not an ordered and structured tale that I shall tell. And my love story — well, it concerns three different ladies and is all wound up with everything else. However, I think that without any additional delay, I should tell of my boyhood and my association with Bladesover House.

There was a time when I thought of Bladesover House as a complete and authentic working model of the entire world. As a small boy, I had great faith in this notion. The great house itself, constructed in French chateau style in the eighteenth century, lay at Bladesover on the Kentish Downs and dominated village, church and the surrounding countryside. Now, it can easily be imagined how the central and overpowering relation of Bladesover House to all that surrounded it might impress me in a way that suggested the great house and its magnificent grounds as the most significant things in the world, with everything else functioning only in relation to them. They represented gentry, authority and quality, and from this great house, servants, laborers, tradesmen and farmfolk seemed to receive their permission to exist. By thirteen or fourteen, some hereditary touch of skepticism surfaced in me, and I even ventured to wonder if Mr. Bartlett, the vicar, knew positively about God. I even went so far as to question the unchallengeable perfection of the gentry and their central position in society. By fourteen the trait had taken hold, and I had been so irregular as to decide to marry the daughter of a viscount and to deposit a black eye upon her half-brother. As I have already said, Bladesover, the town, the church, and the various degrees of laborers, townspeople and servants, struck me as a complete social system. Other villages and estates seemed only to perpetuate this sublimely ordered scheme. I reckoned that London was simply a more magnificent country town and the Queen the most splendid of all gentlefolk. That all this social perfection was even then in the process of deterioration never dawned on me then, so well did my mother advise me of my proper place in the order of things. In fact I was not truly aware of the downward movement of this system even by the time that Tono-

Bungay was in its ascendency. Even today only a scant minority comprehend the fact that this delicately refined hierarchy of pretense has passed from us. The great houses remain, but the grip of change holds the system fast, pausing, as it were, before sweeping it away forever.

Bladesover House, the place where my mother had been housekeeper, was now let full furnished to Sir Reuben Lichenstein. Old Lady Drew had died, and the house, like other fine houses, thereabouts, was put on by new and unlikely tenants like a great but antiquated gown. Hawksnest was owned by a rather slick newspaper proprietor, while Redgrave housed presently a family of brewers. However, on the whole there seemed to be remarkably little difference in all these notable substitutions, for the village about Bladesover appeared about the same — on a visit there a laborer tipped his cap; he was certain he knew his proper place and mine. When I was a boy everyone had a place. It was part of your birthright, and with it came an understanding that there were also your superiors and your inferiors. At the heart of the Bladesover system was Lady Drew, ancient and wizened, and garrulous — a woman whose memory swirled about with a marvelous range of genealogies. With her, too, was old Miss Somerville, cousin and companion, and from the quarters allotted to my mother as housekeeper, I could hear sometimes these two souls above in the parlor, moving about, silent with their two pet dogs and memories of a time when Bladesover swelled with young blades and dazzling ladies, with gaiety and abundant courtliness.

In due course, I was even granted an audience with these Bladesover dieties; for so they seemed to a young boy well schooled in a becoming awareness of place and position. Her Ladyship in black silk pressed a half-crown into my hand and the shrunken hand trembled as she enunciated her wish that I be a good boy. Miss Somerville stood behind, even paler than Lady Drew, with high color in her cheeks and a distinct yellowness to her hair. The secret of that remarkable color of course was made known to us in those intimate conversations held in the housekeeper's rooms. However, after my violent dispute with young Garval, I fell into disfavor, was banished from paradise and never saw those two withered Olympians again.

Within respectable distance of these splendid beings, scattered about the fringes of the sublime, were the vicarage people, those individuals who maintain their own particular corner in the English scheme of things. In the past two hundred years, the vicar of the

English Church has made remarkable social progress; today it is only the Church of England village schoolmaster who has inherited the insignificant social position of the seventeenth-century country parson. In the Bladesover hierarchy, the vicar ranked above the doctor; there were, of course, a grand range of other degrees of social precedence split up among footmen, shopkeepers, sons of this one and that, blacksmiths, butlers, housekeepers and so forth. As for myself, I absorbed this rich tapestry of social significance during my Bladesover days from my mother, from Rabbits, the butler, and from the list of servants and visitors that formed a lesser ladder of importance beneath those perfect beings, shuffling this way and that in the parlor over my mother's quarters. Rising out of all these quaint and curious memories is the image of my mother, whom I knew did not allow me her love because in me she saw more of my father every day. Lady Drew breathed genealogies, but my mother was an expert on "place." She could most confidently identify everyone's proper social place, knew the subtle distinctions existing between peers, the proper etiquette and arrangements for the seating of servants at her tea table—but she was never sure of my father's place, wherever that might have been. Bladesover was good for me. Through it I came to understand many of the mysteries of English society. Two hundred years ago England was one vast Bladesover, but the English have never severed with the system thoroughly, as did the French with their's after the Revolution.

The social status on the servant level perpetuated itself also. Tea was endured for about three quarters of an hour, and the conversation was maddening in its want of variety. The ritual was often held in the housekeeper's quarters my mother occupied, and it was particularly loathsome when several pensioned-off servants were received; namely, Mrs. Mackridge, Mrs. Booch and Mrs. Latude-Fernay, women who seemed large at the time, beaded and swathed in flouncy clothes, launching their disdaining eyes on my youthful restlessness and constructing a maddening pettiness of conversation. During these Bladesover days, I wondered about my father, but even to this day, I do not know whether he is alive or dead. He had left my mother's comfort long before I could remember it, and she on her side had destroyed every reminder of his existence, save her marriage certificate, her wedding ring and me. She never spoke of him, and what I eventually learned came from his brother, and my uncle, Edward Ponderevo. But Bladesover was really a good thing for me. There was an education to be gotten there, not simply in the social way; there were books as well. To be sure, Lady Drew's taste ran to a variety of rubbish; but there had been Sir Cuthbert, son of the man who built the house, whose taste sustained quality. In a large room upstairs were to be discovered a host of treasures, and there it was that I gained familiarity with Hogarth, Thomas Paine, Swift, Voltaire and Gibbon. There was a boyish fuzziness in my acquaintance with them, but I read them through nevertheless. From the upstairs room I invaded the salon, but my boldness was scotched by the head housemaid. Yet, I recollect a translation of Plato's *Republic* and William Beckford's *Vathek*.

The school I attended was allowable under the Bladesover system. Of course the lower classes were not considered to require schooling and the middle level of humanity simply got whatever it got. My recollections of those days are that they were not unhappy ones. There was schoolboy brawling, some uninspired cricket, arithmetic and algebra, and, on the whole, a rather serviceable amount of instruction from our headmaster. We had our good times at that school, and among the most durable of the benefits it provided for me was a lifelong friend in Bob Ewart, the illegitimate son of an improvident artist and himself an artist now — old Ewart, so completely uncommon and so marvelously sensitive and rare an individual. We were inseparable friends, and I wonder just how much of each other's natures we came to share.

My early youth also felt the mark of another remarkable person, the Honorable Beatrice Normandy. I had met her when she was eight and I was nearly twelve. She had been brought by Nannie, her nurse, one of those time-honored servant-nurses who had muffled their own maternal instincts in favor of those stiffly bestowed upon another woman's child. I recall the occasion of our first encounter over tea in my mother's quarters, an occasion when young Beatrice inquired if I were a servant boy and Nannie decided dryly that her charge ought not to speak to me. It was also noticed that my hands were dirty and that my collar was frayed. How I longed at that moment to make the Honorable Beatrice Normandy admire me! Thus our acquaintance began and even deepened somewhat on such occasions when I was permitted to play with her. My manners were even praised by that sentinel Nannie, which pleased both my mother and Lady Drew. And so Beatrice and I would pass playful afternoons in the great doll's house near the nursery. It was a lavish toy, costing a great amount of money, and had been a gift from the Prince Regent to Sir Harry Drew's first child, who had died young. When I returned to school, my mind was alive with beautiful thoughts, and I persuaded Ewart to talk to me about life.

It was after my fourteenth birthday that the moment of disgrace occurred. I had seen Beatrice and her half-brother Archie Garvell several times during my final holiday at Bladesover, but I cannot recollect the first meeting with Archie. I do know that we despised each other, this haughty boy and I, and that it was an instinctive thing. I know also that I loved Beatrice; even at fourteen I loved her. I love *you*, she had said to me, and I don't love Archie, and we had kissed and embraced eagerly. And when the three of us played it was I who directed the make-believe instead of Garvell, for I had outread him tenfold and so had a keener knowledge of just how our play should be carried out. On the infamous occasion I wished to be a Spanish nobleman, and Archie was to be an entire tribe of Indians. He would hear none of it. It would not do; it would be impossible for me to play a gentleman since I was not one. Beatrice did not care, but Archie was firm. It was only when he ridiculed me for dropping the H's in my words that I attacked him. He had some style, but I had fought before with bare knuckles. Some style was all he had, like so much of the English upper class that quibbles over form and feeble points of honor and claims credit without ever having really come to grips with anything. However, we were caught in the act of thumping each other by Lady Drew and Miss Somerville. Beatrice, who had cheered the brawling, now fled to Her Ladyship in feigned horror, and Archie rose to the occasion with charges of unfair and dishonorable tactics on my part. How did I dare? cried Lady Drew —and so I was banished from Bladesover. I did smart at the fact that the Honorable Beatrice Normandy denied me, but to this day I do not regret having given young Garvell such a solid thrashing.

COMMENT: It has been noted previously in this guide that Henry James had remarked on similarities between Wells and the novelist Charles Dickens. In *The Invisible Man* certain descriptions of the comical countryfolk are surely Dickensian. In *The War of the Worlds,* Wells's portraits of frantic crowds of humanity are remarkably similar to Dickens' in power to capture the tension and visual horror of mobs. Here in the beginning of *Tono-Bungay,* Wells is Wells; but he is so remarkably Dickensian, too. There is in the book as a whole something of the spirit of Dickens' *David Copperfield* or *Great Expectations,* a spirit in which a young boy moves upward across a social canvas amid comic, painful and very often outlandish circumstances. This first chapter bears a resemblance to *Great Expectations* as far as the characters that Wells has created. In Dickens, eccentrics abound, and their eccentricities are even excessive. Wells's characters are quaint but do not assume a grotesque eccentricity as do those of Dickens. In *Great Expectations* there is old Miss Haversham, wrinkled, aristocratic, lonely and imperious. There is the boy Pip, and the haughtily cruel girl Estella with whom the young Pip falls in love. It is possible, then, to detect certain similarities between Miss Haversham and Lady Drew, Estella and Beatrice Normandy, Pip and Master George Ponderevo. What similarity is present rests on the initial impression of quaintness in Well's Bladesover people, but they are not drawn deeply into Dickensian type eccentricity, and their shapes do not approximate the comic or grimly grotesque. The nearest Wells comes to a Dickensian grotesque is in his brief but colorful engagement of the Frapp family in the following chapter.

Both Dickens and Wells turned a harshly appraising eye toward society. Even in this initial chapter, Wells is at the throat of the English social scheme: the Bladesover system—a preposterous inheritance of values placing individuals along a chain of social being—every man with a proper place, and in that place. And the symbol for this is Lady Drew herself, old, cracked and dried like parchment, her mind cluttered with webs of genealogical lines, and waiting in her upper parlor to die, as surely, Wells is saying, as the system she represents is dying. Lady Drew, a stiffened matriarchal figure, from whom the shadow of place and proper position has extended over servants, across the lands about Bladesover, and even to the commonest laborer.

The English gentry and their social proprieties take as hard a thrashing in this first chapter as young Ponderevo administers to Archie Garvell. And young Garvell perhaps, as much as anyone in Chapter I, receives the literal and figurative blows that Wells lets fly at the upper class England of his day. Young Beatrice Normandy, haughty and spirited, betrays some promising democratic qualities at times; but in the end she is true to her "place," true to the system that recognizes young Ponderevo as beneath her. The reader should not forget this willful little girl, for Wells is far from disposing of her as a character, and she will be reintroduced significantly later in the novel.

CHAPTER II

At my removal from Bladesover, my mother despatched me to the home of her cousin Nicodemus Frapp; later, I was sent to my Uncle, Edward Ponderevo. The Frapps were innocuous souls, the master of the house being without initiative in his baking business and without pride in his appearance; his wife was a plump creature who avoided physical exertion at all cost. "Uncle" Frapp had never mounted an assault against the world, and a resignation to God's will served as a convenient shelter for whatever befell him. The Frapps were slovenly, without a book in the house, and their only activity was a Sunday hymn meeting with other grubby and unclean souls, all equally confident of the deserved Glory that would be theirs in the hereafter. My mother paid them ten shillings a week for me, and for this I slept with the two older Frapp children, passing my days in the chaos of the Frapp bakehouse and in periodic deliveries of bread.

The house of Frapp was a dreadful place, and whenever possible I got out into the streets of Chatham and walked about its unrelieved squalor and dinginess. It presented itself as the very opposite of Bladesover. One could gather that since Bladesover was *really* what England was all about, then anyone who did not fit properly into the Bladesover spectrum was, therefore, gotten off into places such as this, to rot, and to give thanks even for that privilege. That, it could be believed, must be the scheme of it all.

On one particular night while abed with my cousins Frapp, I thrust upon them my doubts and disbeliefs concerning revealed religion, matters which Ewart and I had once developed. There is no Hell and no ever-lasting punishment, I declared. They were scandalized and dumfounded. The next day "Uncle" Frapp prayed for me, but I certainly did not expect to have that Sunday's prayer meeting open fire upon me. They marshalled their forces; I was badgered with chapter and verse by those reverent souls—but I held out staunchly. These people were bullying me into an atheism that terrified me. When I learned that the next meeting would be no different than this one, I left the Frapp household early on that day of inquisition and made for Bladesover. On the way I grew ever more doubtful about the nature of my reception, but I pressed on nonetheless. Once at Bladesover, I secluded myself and finally intercepted my mother returning from church. I gave her a start, to be sure, but I proceeded to explain that I would drown myself rather than return to Chatham and the Frapp family. It was by third-class carriage that my mother then took me to Wimblehurst and my uncle Edward Ponderevo, my father's brother. He must be about twenty-seven or so, she said; he was called Teddy when he was younger. And Teddy he was, indeed, when I saw him; in fact one might say there was a particular Teddiness about him. He was quick, without suggesting intelligence or gracefulness. His face was full, and there were the unmistakable early signs of a potbelly in the making.

In the window of his chemist shop was a sign boldly soliciting the populace to buy Ponderevo's Cough Linctus NOW. Cheaper now than in winter, it read; this was the time to put in a supply.

The quarters my uncle shared with his wife, my aunt Susan, were small and stuffy. They would never rival Bladesover, but they seemed a wonderful relief from the establishment of the Frapps. My aunt Susan was a slender pretty woman at the time, about twenty-three or four with fine blue eyes and a clear wholesome complexion. My mother announced that she had brought me and then proceeded to make small talk about my uncle's apartment and his business. Oh, it's adequate, and the shop goes along somehow, he replied, but it's not at all what I should have—and the town—well, the town is dead, room for growth. Someday, he may have a bounty, and it will be just too much for him, replied my aunt Susan with wry affection.

I sat and watched the exchange, and I was taken by the humorous sparkle in my uncle's eye, the glasses which ill-fitted his nose, and the curious way he had, at times, of half-whistling by drawing the air between his teeth. So, when they had excused me to walk about the town, to avoid my hearing what they had to say of my father, it was decided that I should remain there with my uncle as a sort of chemist's apprentice. I was to live there, and incredibly enough I was to learn Latin. I had recognized the disadvantage in not having studied Latin when it was thrust upon me by the priggish Archie Garvell, but my reading at Bladesover emphasized the fact as well. I have always wanted to learn Latin, I said. My mother replied that I was to learn it not because I wanted to, but because I had to.

When I parted from my mother at the train that day, there was a disturbing gentleness in her manner. She embraced me possessively. In her strictness, in her fearful narrowness, she told me to be good and not to defy my betters, those who were above me. I did not realize then that this was to be the last time I would ever see tears in my mother's eyes. It was not long after that she died, and it was only at the funeral that I realized her severity and starch had only belied a deep love for me. I had been the only thing she loved, and it was not until the moment of her burial that I understood this—not until this moment that I could love her fully. Certainly, I could not prevent the tears that flowed so freely upon these thoughts.

CHAPTER III
The Wimblehurst Apprenticeship

At my uncle's chemist shop in Wimblehurst, I set about learning my Latin and what I could of materia medica. I had been used to the wide authority of Bladesover House, but in Wimblehurst the authority of Estry House was even wider, extending as it did over an entire borough—certainly a more thoroughgoing example of the eighteenth-century system than Bladesover. But my uncle Edward Ponderevo represented for me the first living contradiction of the Bladesover system; the Frapps in their insufficiency and incompetence had only served to strengthen my early impressions about the rightness of the Bladesover order of things. Wimblehurst, dead, dead!, my uncle would cry as we checked stock. Somewhere, things are happening. George, he would say. Not here—Lord Estry gets his though—up in London, or in America—the market—get a corner—take a flyer—Oh Lord!—no end to things once you think about it. And he would suddenly whistle through his teeth—Zzzzz. Rush about—get things done—Oh, I *must* do something—why did I ever settle here?—And Lord Estry—does he want any change?—never, any change means a loss for him—Zzzz.

So I remember my uncle Edward Ponderevo in these early years; restless, eager, talkative, and growing a bit fleshy with time. As for myself, I proceeded with my studies, learning my Latin and taking government-sponsored mathematics and mechanical drawing classes with application and enthusiasm. My exercise consisted mostly of walking, since I did not take well to the youths about Wimblehurst, loutish, shallow, and insufferably self-contented in their limitations. I am a staunch believer that the English townsman, even in his slums, is more capable spiritually and imaginatively than the lad from the countryside. At my boarding school of Goudhurst with such people as Ewart, we had our coarse moments, but above it all was an undefinable richness of romantic imagination. At Wimblehurst the youth was base—low, without the relief of wit; lewd, without a literate escape. I gained no friends among the young men of the neighborhood, nor did I experience any love affairs that I might recount here. Desire I could not deny, but love was always something that encouraged shyness—it was, I think, my role always to be the ineffectual lover. In those days my slender and delicate aunt Susan was the one who captured my attention with her sweet half-maternal ways. I was busy and I wrote to Ewart when I could, but my uncle played a major role in my educational impressions—and, of course, in my discontent with Wimblehurst. But the warmest of relationships was with my aunt with her wistfully humorous way of prefixing things with "old"—the old newspapers—and that old sardine, uncle. She was a loving and sweetly humorous person, and it seems to me that her chief occupation in life was to make my uncle laugh with some new nickname. And when he did laugh, what a wonderfully snorting and windy thing it was! Despite the warmth of our family relationship in Wimblehurst, both my uncle and aunt were socially separated from the rest of the town, with my uncle Teddy as the butt of jokes—going to build Wimblehurst into a thundering enterprise, they are, someone would cry our sarcastically at him. A scourge before that would ever happen, he would hurl back.

It was my uncle's scientific approach to the stock market that ruined him in Wimblehurst. By the time we were forced to leave Wimblehurst, to the ridicule of the shopkeepers, I came to realize that Teddy Ponderevo had used the better part of the six hundred pounds my mother had entrusted to him for me as part of his sure stroke of fortune in the market. And yet I felt so sorry for him, almost as much as I did for Aunt Susan. I knew then, I suppose, that he was *weaker* than I, as incorrigibly irresponsible and romantically giddy as I would know him to be on the day of his death. I'm not without offers—London, you know, he said. A hundred to one it was, George. The trick is to keep some back. The next day I would have been back in the market and caught the rise—chance—chance —it's a lesson to me.

When they were forced to leave the chemist shop in Wimblehurst, my uncle was a bit too plucky to be believable—and my aunt in her wistfully humorous way said I should write when they finally made me a professor. As they drove off, Aunt Susan held my eyes for a moment, her own wide and glistening, while the knowing shopkeepers nearby exchanged self-satisfied glances about just desserts for the improvident Teddy Ponderevo. Mr. Mantell was the new proprietor in the Wimblehurst chemist shop, and with his occupancy, I turned more devotedly to my science studies—chemistry, physiology, heat, light, geology—absorbed for the most part from poorly written and abbreviated textbooks. Then, having outrun the requirements of the Pharmaceutical Society's examination, and being younger than the legal application age of twenty-one, I set out to assault a Bachelor of Science degree at London University. I was nineteen years of age.

When I came to London I made my way through the cosmopolitan maze to Tottenham Court Road and the pharmacy that my uncle managed. He seemed shorter now as he met me warmly—and he seemed a bit rounder as well. Aunt Susan was not quite as slender as she had been, I thought, but her complexion was as fresh as ever. She still, however, poked fun at my uncle, and I was glad to see that the habit persisted. Their quarters were common and uninspiring, and I was struck by the unintelligent reality of an intelligent populace living in such inadequate second-rate housing; they were of early Victorian origin, but now it was like the wearing of used clothing. And the drudgery of these places, and the people in them; they were honest and useful, not fitting in any way into the whole Bladesover scheme of things. No one was concerned about decent and civilized housing for these people—the squeeze was on, and the landlords always made out well.

My uncle, stimulated by the idea that I had never seen London, marched me about with authority. Over tea, my uncle informed my aunt Susan that I was going to make my fortune in electricity. I would be content with less, I replied, and my aunt in her funning way, remarked that she and my uncle Teddy were certain to make theirs—however, he had not told her exactly when it should come about. Zzzz, said my uncle, a woman doesn't understand about time in these things. It was then that he introduced me to Tono-Bungay—and when he mentioned it, I was not certain it was the name of anything. Just wait, he said—just wait—Tono-Bungay. That was positively all I could extract from him.

When I had left my aunt and uncle that evening, I was depressed by the awareness of shabby mediocrity in the lives they were leading. I thought of his dreamy flights into elegance and the threadbare cuffs he wore—I am to ride in a fine carriage, my aunt would say with a smile. It was January. It was my first visit to London, and I had been depressed by it. I doubted my uncle, and I feared for him and my aunt Susan—I was to learn differently.

COMMENT: In Book I, we have seen Wells lash out in several directions. He has scored the English social system sharply with its gross manifestation in Bladesover House and those who are associated with it. Lady Drew is a shriveled relic of a decaying system—an eighteenth-century system of big house and dependent town and territory. In his mother, George Ponderevo sees the servant-class embodiment of the Bladesover scheme, a woman who maintains a lifelong consciousness of place, understanding full well those that are beneath her, and accepting without challenge the fact that there are those who are above her and are her betters. I know my place, her person seems to cry out to the very last. Young George Ponderevo seems to be ever in conflict with the system and in his encounter with Archie Garvell, the voice of Wells breaks through to touch the shallow insubstantial character of the English upper class. The Frapp family is comic to be sure, but in their lethargic ignorance, dragging themselves from one end of life to the other, they are revolting as well. Equally as condemnable in Wells's eyes is their smug satisfaction in an assurance of eternal glory, a curious sense of complacent superiority over the more intelligent, more industrious and more able in life. For them the vision of eternal reward makes the wretchedness of their life, their ineffectuality, and their astounding failure as human beings almost a sweetly justifiable burden. With Teddy Ponderevo, Wells finds a challenger to the Bladesover system. Teddy does not recognize his "place" as do the other shopkeepers in Wimblehurst. He is all for rising in the world, for getting in on affairs. His restless dreaming of financial triumphs, and his stock market blunder that cost him his chemist shop and his nephew's inheritance, may seem improvident at first, but the as yet undisciplined will to rise in the world is a healthy social sign. It hammers at the caste system of Bladesover and represents the energy of a new ascendent class, one without Lady Drew's genealogies and refined sense of position, an ingenious self-made commercial class whose influence is great and whose power is money.

It is impossible not to compare Nichodemus Frapp and his wife with Teddy and Susan Ponderevo. The Frapps are no better than they should be, slovenly in appearance and in business, ill-equipped for real living, and unworthy of a worthwhile survival of life's challenges. In its benevolence, the social scheme has awarded Teddy Ponderevo a strictly limited horizon, like the Bladesover Olympians patronizing the less blessed. But Teddy Ponderevo in his dreams and false starts has driven a wedge in the system that Tono-Bungay will finally breach. Beside Ponderevo's bubbling ambitions, the wrinkled grandeur of Lady Drew appears even more lifeless than it is.

In this first book, Wells takes good aim at the English educational system. He remarks on the use of poorly written and condensed textbooks. As a boy he longed to learn Latin and when the opportunity presented itself as a chemist's apprentice to his uncle, his mother remarked that he would learn it because he *had* to and not because he wanted to—education, it seems, was to be a labored and painful duty, if it were to be proper at all. Education of course was basically for the upper class, the middle classes being grateful for what they received of it—while the lower classes, by their very position, were held to be incompatible with the notion at all.

If the reader is periodically distracted by Wells the social critic, the development of character in this first book should not be ignored. In particular, it is Aunt Susan who should be observed carefully. If Teddy Ponderevo is ebullient and high spirited, he is beautifully balanced by his wife, Susan, gently, ironically witty, with smiles carefully balanced on the edge of melancholy. Patient and faithful, she abides Teddy's flights with a loving skepticism that never rules out her belief in the possibility of their success. She is a wonderful character, and Wells will develop her into a thoroughly beautiful one by the end of the novel.

BOOK THE SECOND
The Rise of Tono-Bungay

CHAPTER I
How I Became A London Student and Went Astray

When I was twenty-two I came to live in London. Every day, more and more impressions of the city were added to my mind until, gradually, I saw a certain pattern or structure to it. Bladesover, for me, had been the pattern for all England. The splendid gentry that inhabited Bladesover and Estry may no longer be there, but they have been replaced by the financial and mercantile giants—the inhabitants may have changed, but the general character of the system is much the same. One encountered Olympians here and there, and it was indeed possible to mark out the area in London where the great houses and their inhabitants stood.

When I came to London that year, I was quite open-minded, and very eager. I wanted so to be productive and to accomplish—and not simply settle for happiness. I had come to London on a scholarship in mechanics and metallurgy and hoped it would lead me into engineering. When I arrived I was certain that the discipline and industry I had shown in my studies at Wimblehurst would support me here. Unfortunately, they did not. At Wimblehurst, my scientific abilities had seemed exceptional to the inhabitants—here in London, I was reduced to insignificance. London made me aware of so much I had never known—fresh impressions and unending opportunities. I did not, however, apply myself properly to my studies.

It was near Highgate Hill, though, that I finally came upon Ewart in his shabby artist's lodgings. Well, he said, after a while—science for you and sculpture for me. Life was perplexing for him, Ewart said:

sex and dissipation, the desire to work artistically and then the yearning to break off whatever was begun. I just don't see why I'm here, he said, or where it is that I come into the scheme of things. On the whole, Ewart's conversation made me aware of a basic adventurous quality to life, but emphasized what I had already felt—a sense of purposelessness in London life, a want of objectives in the lives of people about us. We walked then and talked of theology and philosophy, and I got my first encounter with socialism.

We met often after that and discovered his own concept of the general vagueness of life. This suited his native lethargy, but I was all for action in life. From Ewart came the seeds of my socialistic thought and yet, it was I who had to rouse him to action. Get out and join some organization, I said—social action. A visit to a Fabian Society meeting was totally unrewarding with its mixture of vague theories, inconclusive discussions and rambling speeches.

The idea of socialism occupied much of my thinking; but since my days in Wimblehurst, a greater awareness of the other sex had been growing as well. By now, I was tasting of what life might be like by falling in love, somewhat, with girls I would pass on the street, with actresses, or women I might see in tea shops or on the corner. It is certainly strange, though, that I cannot recollect just when it was that I first saw Marion. I married Marion, and as events proved, we were only to heap misery upon each other's lives. I had seen her coming and going at the art museum and was struck by the graceful loveliness of her form and the stark simplicity in her way of dressing. Our early conversations were, as I recall, woefully average and lifeless, and those first few encounters only half-accidental. Her thoughts were uninspired, but this did not bother me, for it was her physical presence that had a grip on my attention. Love, I thought, would lie ahead. She gained a great hold upon me, though, and the physical attraction she had for me was strong enough to disallow whatever imperfections of face and figure I detected in her.

I met her mother, father and aunt in their drab and tasteless home in Walham Green. The Ramboats were dull people. The mother was once pretty but seemed worn now. Mr. Ramboat's eyes offered only unintelligence, and in his retirement he now occupied himself with a small garden out back.

My passion for Marion grew progressively, and I devoted more and more time and thought to her. She was ignorant; that I knew—but there was a fineness and a pure simplicity about her that rendered her defects trivial. I recall telling her that I loved her, of trying to put my arm about her. Love me? she said, bewildered and unprepared. I kissed her, and she seemed paralysed in unresponse. Never again, she said, never do that again. I wanted to marry her, I said, but she objected with a frightened coolness. Love — to marry — it all seemed to terrify her — to be beyond her imagination, and she could not handle the idea at all.

My studies fell to pieces, and I had little money left. In bitterness, I wrote to my uncle, half threatening about my mother's money he had lost for me and had made no effort to return. Academically, I was a failure; but then who among the brightest students, or even the professors, have accomplished what I have? Had I been trained in the investigation of myopic academic trivia, would I have built the undreamed-of boats I have? — would I have had a fellowship in the Royal Society by the age of thirty-seven? However, at that time, I had been in London for two years, was overwhelmed with frustration for Marion, and had made a sorry bungle of my studies.

CHAPTER II
The Dawn Comes, and My Uncle Appears in a New Silk Hat

I had avoided seeing my uncle throughout my student days, for I still bridled at having been deprived of monies that were rightfully mine. Then I saw that soon to be famous name on a billboard — TONO-BUNGAY. I was trying to recall where I had heard it before when my uncle's telegram arrived and summoned me to him and Tono-Bungay. When I finally discovered his shop on Raggett Street, he met me at full tilt — George, he cried, Tono-Bungay — bellow it out — let everyone know now — Tono-Bungay — it's afloat — going strong. My uncle had a new silk hat and a frock coat with satin lapels and off we went to lunch at Schaffer's with its respectful waiters who seemed to know him. Know me already, they do, he said — can recognize a comer — selling marvelously. Put it together out of old recipe books, he continued, stimulating and aromatic and intoxicating, too, you know. After lunch, Uncle Teddy Ponderevo puffed a cigar and waxed exuberant. He had gotten others to invest when he himself had nothing. There was, of course, that matter of your inheritance, he said, and I should have put it right — but George — it's afloat now — and it's turned out properly. I was to have three hundred pounds a year to come in with him. He had confidence in me — always had — and needed me now to help make it go — Zzzz. I replied that the whole thing sounded like a swindle and that dishonesty was unnecessary to make a living. No fraud in it, said my uncle, but think about it and come to our new lodgings in Gower street on Sunday.

It took a week for me to surrender to the Tono-Bungay scheme. I walked about looking at the impressive advertisements of the great commercial products — and didn't some of their creators sit in Parliament? A visit to Ewart brought no moral strength to me, whatsoever. But then there was Marion. I told her once again that I wanted to marry her, but her response was as dryly unyielding as ever. I felt a quick spasm of antagonism toward her for a moment, and it was unfortunate that I did not discover in it a basic antagonism between us that lay concealed there. There's just no use in marrying, she said at last . . . what good in it . . . a little money at best . . . or maybe no money . . . and children, too. Yes, she said, after I had spoken, it *could* be done on three hundred a year . . . others do it on less. It seems that at that moment we became engaged, and I look back now on my noticeable boyishness about the whole thing. When I went at last to my uncle's address on Gower Street, I was greeted by my aunt who had tea waiting for him. There was a stately grandeur about the furnishings, almost a hint of Bladesover, and in addition, my aunt and uncle had a serving maid. Aunt Susan related how my uncle had been bubbling over and finally gotten the Tono-Bungay thing "afloat." He needs you in it, George, she said, says he can't make it last and keep steady without you. But it's trash, I objected. It's our only chance, she replied. Suddenly, my uncle had arrived and burst into the room. Well, George, he said, are you in? Yes, I answered, and there won't be any more hesitations. I kept my word on that score — for seven years, to be exact.

COMMENT: George Ponderevo, against his better judgment, decided in favor of the Tono-Bungay enterprise. He has floundered in his studies, carried away somewhat by London itself, his philosophical conversations with the Bohemian Ewart, and his passion for the dull and inhibited Marion Ramboat. He is really unsure of just what he believes. He is drawn to socialism and social theory, but his responses to sex, capitalism, poverty and the latitudes of free enterprise are not clearly defined as yet. Furthermore, his judgment is often hampered by his urgent desire for Marion. This, plus the expectation of marrying her on three hundred pounds a year, combines with his affection for his aunt and uncle to bring him into the colossal promotion of this fraudulent elixir.

CHAPTER III
How We Made Tono-Bungay Hum

And so, together, my uncle and I began to sell this bottled humbug. It was his genius for promoting that did it all, though. He wrote his own advertisements that exuded confidence, sincerity and profound concern for the consumer's health. We both worked hard, I must say, and it had something of the flavor of a game for me as I poured my enthusiasm into the promotion of the thing. We branched out, too, with Tono-Bungay Hair Stimulant, Tono-Bungay Lozenges and Tono-Bungay Chocolate. Zzzz, he would say, the romance of modern commerce, and he proceeded to bring out Tono-Bungay Mouthwash and to spread our territories throughout Great Britain. I contributed my part, too, with the addition of a type of automatic production line with filling, capping and machine labeling done in a neat sequence. We developed greater efficiency in our packing methods as well. As for credit, there was not the slightest difficulty in obtaining one hundred fifty thousand pounds when we needed it. Remarkable it was, and can you conceive of the lunacy in a world that would finance and nourish such a sham?

I had brought Ewart into the office for a poster we had in mind. *The* problem in life, he expounded to my uncle, was that we are never really alive, even though we want to be, never in the fullest sense . . . never truly alive. The poetry of commerce, he raved on, your nephew just doesn't seem to see it. Yes, said my uncle, we are both artists, you and I, and it's advertisement that's done it for me . . . will do it for the whole world, will revolutionize the world . . . it will, someday. But your modern commerce is merciful, said Ewart. It resurrects. It takes things, raises them up, transforms them like Cana . . . water into Tono-Bungay . . . why, you'd make the dust respect itself. For a moment my uncle did not quite know how to interpret what Ewart was raving about, but passed it off with a puff of his cigar. Clever fellow, that one, he said later, but a bit drunk.

Ewart's efforts at a poster came to nought. He did produce one, however, in a spasm of irony; a picture of two beavers looking remarkably like my uncle and I, beneath which was the legend, "Modern Commerce."

CHAPTER IV
Marion

I was twenty-four when I married Marion Ramboat, about a year after Tono-Bungay was well under way, and it was not until a host of conflicts and objections had gotten in the way. Actually, Marion and I never really shared a single idea, and there was also that vein of antagonism that remained. We did share a certain mutual ignorance about some things, but what maintained our attachment for one another was my passion for her physical beauty and the appeal that my high regard had for her. She was, however, always a girl who was conscious of her class. Ours was certainly a mismatch and a markedly wrong love relationship; it strikes me now as amazing that in such an important thing as this, something that truly affects the future of generations, that our society should have its couples unite in such a clumsy, chancy, and childishly ignorant manner. My own sexual development was not unusual. I was never told anything; nothing was ever explained, and what I gathered came with an uncertainty and in attendance with restriction and apprehension. Scraps were all I had gathered, and I assembled these as best I could through instinct and the fertility of a romantic imagination. For Marion, it was a matter of repression. Her want of education regarding the natural function of sex in marriage had not rendered her shy in these concerns, but rather impossible. For her it was a horrible function of life and something that she did not wish to think of, or respond to, for as long as she could avoid doing so.

Smithie was in her thirties, thin with thrusting teeth, and good natured. At her cloth cutting tables where Marion worked, it could be learned from the other girls that a fiancé was not to be taken lightly and that he should be held on to. Smithie was a likeable soul, but at the time I detested her. After our marriage, she was often at our house, and she exerted a much stronger influence upon Marion than I did. For me, Marion was never to catch fire. I am forty-five now, and I can reflect upon those days. We were both victims, it seems. Certainly, I did not bring understanding to bear, only the unreasonable force of passion.

It was only when I announced that I was to get five hundred pounds a year and that we should have a house at Ealing that Marion agreed to a more foreseeable time for marriage. However, after interminable haggling over the place and the details of the ceremony, I slammed the door and said I was through with the entire business. I saw Ewart soon afterwards, and he discoursed on the public morality. All hypocrisy; secret sinning; youth prevented from finding out; ignorance for adolescence and sexual blundering in maturity. After some days I received a note from Marion confessing her selfishness, and so we were married. At the wedding my aunt Susan was both observant and attentive. She looked at Marion and strained to see the marks of love that she herself had experienced. I had not told my aunt and uncle about Marion until a few days before the wedding; even at the wedding, it was most difficult to talk to my aunt about her.

The wedding over, the honeymoon followed and it was, in its final analysis, a failure. I shall not belabor the subject further. As for the marriage itself, rather than flower into a warm and private intimacy, it chose to be a compromising exchange of baby talk in which I was "Mutney" and Marion was "Ming." They were dull, insipid hours we passed together. Her tastes were almost devotedly plain. She was narrow without the slightest range of imagination, and she wore the blinders of her class without pause. It was unfortunate, too, that she and my aunt Susan never got on. My aunt's warmth and openness, a sort of maternal overflow, were met by a taut defensiveness on Marion's part and an unwavering misinterpretation of wit for ridicule. Our marriage grew narrower, more arduous, too, and Marion fearfully rejected the idea of motherhood. The end of our union came at last with my own infidelity—with Effie Rink, one of the typists in our Raggett Street office. Smithie's brother had seen us at our rendezvous and had told Marion. I felt no shame, but rather annoyance at the discovery. Oddly enough, it was after the whole business was out in the open that any sort of a tenderness sprang up between us. The shock of the thing had actually animated her. It was only for a few days, but it was the one time we ever truly reached one another—and then it was over. There was, at last, talk of divorce and alimony, and it was with extreme effort that I steeled myself against the effect of this new Marion who had come alive. At last she pleaded with me not to leave. Mutney, she cried, I'll be alone . . . I didn't understand . . . In my determination, I would not yield to speculations of how this marriage might endure if I remained. I had, of course, committed myself to Effie.

And so I went to Effie, who never fought to get Marion out of my distressed memory. For a time I even considered an effort at reconciliation with Marion, but I could never have returned to the old narrow tasteless ways of living together again. I also wondered just how many men there had been whose lives were such directionless things, so aimless as mine was. I even contemplated suicide, but I turned instead to salvation, not in the religious sense, however. Out of this dark night of my soul, I turned to science. I also turned to my uncle and told him I was tired of all this hokum, this labored deception — but I have an idea I want to get my teeth into, I said — flying. Flying? he said. Yes, I replied, and I believe it's possible in our time. Much like an indulgent father, my uncle assigned me some capital, shortened some of my duties, and so my work with soaring and flying machines began in earnest. I detect in science, though, the basics of my life, the seeking and dissatisfaction. But what I seek in science touches on the spiritual as well. I do not even know what it is, nor what it resembles. It is something durable and lovely and I pursue it, but it has never been truly within my grasp.

I should say something here of my final contacts with Marion. We corresponded for a while regarding necessary business affairs, and gradually her letters trailed off. She did, however, go into business with Smithie. Eight years came and went, and after a significantly long period without hearing from Marion, I wrote to her and inquired if things went well. She had remarried. I do not know if she even is alive today.

My liaison with Effie ended in due course, as there was never anything built for permanence between us. She married, too, some abominable drug-ridden poet. She was twice his age. But let me return to the progress of Tono-Bungay, my uncle's affairs, and what they accomplished for me.

COMMENT: Book II is worth examining. Wells has compartmentalized something that by its nature is not usually set off by itself in a novel. It is almost as though the unhappy marriage was something necessary to come to grips with in the tale, but something to be over and done with in the narrative. Wells was married in 1891 to a cousin, a girl who emphasized a lengthy engagement period and reserved to herself the decision as to when he was earning sufficient money for them to marry. Approximately two years after their marriage, Wells left his wife and took up residence with a biological student named Amy Robbins. His first marriage to his cousin ended in divorce; and after having been married to Amy and fathering two sons by her, he requested that she consent to his promiscuity. In Marion Ramboat there is an obvious parallel with Wells's first marriage. In his liaison with Effie Rink and divorce from Marion, we can discover biographical support in Wells's own divorce and in his affair with Amy Robbins.

In Book II, moreover, there is much significant commentary on late Victorian sexual mores. Certainly, the ruin of George and Marion's marriage is foretold years before in the secretive, unhealthy attitude of society toward marital sex, smothering the natural and transforming it into a nightmare for marriage partners. Marion, frigid, psychologically inhibited, and terrified by the physical side of marriage, avoids that union as long as possible by prolonging the engagement indefinitely, and by reducing their married life to the babyish endearments of playing house. George is unafraid of marriage, but his ignorance of his role is as lamentable as Marion's own fearful repression. Instinct and an imaginative spirit are the marital assets George brings to his marriage—clumsy and demanding, he only causes the gap to widen between them. The fault is society's, cries Wells, for muffling the significant and the beautiful in shabby ignorance and dirty whispers. What should be lovely and warmly personal becomes sordid and disappointing. This is, however, a section in which George Ponderevo crosses from emotional instability to dedication and direction in life. There is a purging of George here, and he has a purer commitment as we enter Book III.

BOOK THE THIRD
The Great Days of Tono-Bungay

CHAPTER I
The Hardingham Hotel, and How We Became Big People

As Tono-Bungay became a fat property, Edward Ponderevo rounded out, too, and mostly about the equatorial area. His nose seemed to jut out more forcefully now; there was his cigar, of course, and the elegant cosmopolitan manner of his dress. Some of his Wimblehurst simplicities never left him, though, even at the zenith of his fortunes. He always did without a manservant, and he Zzzz'd less now. He did, however, add a secretary and a chauffeur to his life. Tono-Bungay was diversifying more and more, and a partnership with Moggs Soap ensued. Young Moggs's inclinations were to refinement and culture, and so he did not mind being made rich by my uncle's promotional genius, just so long as he was not disturbed. Then, my uncle set to work concocting an impressive historical lineage for the ancestral Moggs, and his enterprise and revolutionary style of marketing made young Moggs, and us, considerably wealthier. There were more acquisitions and more development and promotions, and we eventually launched Domestic Utilities, Do Ut, our second flotation.

There is no need to examine the details of these expansions here, for they have all been recorded in the bankruptcy proceedings and in my own depositions made after my uncle's death. The establishment of Household Services was a crowning achievement for my uncle, and in the process he acquired even more businesses and properties. He was paying out more dividends than he should have, just to maintain it at a promised level. I was not that closely aware of all this since I was engaged at the time with my soaring experiment, and

I hoped soon to have powered flight. But the enterprises of Edward Ponderevo piled higher and higher and grew more shaky and unwieldy, and I never really recognized the instability of it all until it was far too late. He had created an incredible illusion, and the public had paid him lavishly for maintaining it.

In the days of his supremacy, Edward Ponderevo held financial court in the Hardingham Hotel, hearing an infinity of petitions and propositions from an army of concoctors and disposing of each offer with a simple affirmation or denial. But then there was Gordon-Nasmyth and the quap on Mordet Island — quap, in strange mounds of metallic and organic matter alive with deadly radiation. Fifteen hundred per cent interest Gordon-Nasmyth guaranteed — six thousand pounds from you would do, he said; it's there to be taken — illegal to remove it, but it can be done. Some inquiries later proved Nasmyth's estimate of the quap's value to be rather accurate. A sample of quap proved to contain an extremely valuable mineral for use in filaments, and my uncle and I kept this counsel to ourselves. But the quap adventure hung in my mind, and I talked of it often with Gordon-Nasmyth when he came up to see the gliders I was building at Crest Hill. My uncle then bought two periodicals, one a significant critical publication of arts and letters. It was soon humbled when patent medicines were worked in with aesthetics.

COMMENT: The seeds of the Ponderevo downfall have been sown. The financial colossus begun on Tono-Bungay has overflowed its boundaries and has spread to a tasteless exercise of his genius at exploitation, a tidal wave of commercial advertising and merchandising. But the lust to build higher and mightier is out of control and the makings of ultimate disaster are even now beyond the control of this loveable and paunchy wizard with silk hat and cigar.

CHAPTER II
Our Progress from Camden Town to Crest Hill

With the house at Beckenham, my aunt Susan once again became part of a social structure, having been rudely extracted from her Wimblehurst setting some time before. There were garden parties and at-homes, to be sure, but my recollection of the Beckenham natives is one of basic shallowness and high pretense. The women were far from intellectual, and the truth of it is that they had nothing

of any significance to say, and so were impossible conversational-
ists. After the house at Beckenham, there was the Chiselhurst mansion where the socially ascendant were convincingly in evidence.
My uncle was often socially clumsy but my aunt Susan rescued him
as often, and was herself lovingly ill at ease. My uncle, of course,
took great bounds toward gentility, and it seems to me that those
commercially prosperous people, upper-middle classes, I suppose,
have for the past twenty-odd years been edging themselves most
determinedly into that smoothly oiled sophistication.

We were the newly rich, invading the upper levels of society now
and learning poise as well. We were economically and socially on
the rise. And then, of course, the *nouveau riche* begin to shop. They
advance to the appreciation of superb automobiles. In time they
exercise their newly won tastes in the selection of rare books . . .
and then there are the great paintings. My uncle was a dynamic
spender in the last few years before the collapse. Pictures were
bought and commissioned, old clocks purchased, and he bought
wildly and with a distinct passion for the act. My aunt Susan,
though, was never compelled by the pride of possessions. In a way
she became more and more detached as the momentum increased
and the pyramid of wealth and power grew.

Then, Edward Ponderevo bought Lady Grove, that magnificent
house of thirteenth-century origin with its Tudor improvements. Of
old Catholic ownership, its roll of lawn and stone battlements had
now fallen into the grasp of Edward Ponderevo, made worthy by the
ascendency of Tono-Bungay. For the new owners there was, of
course, the necessary meeting with the vicar and his family. We sat
in basket chairs on their lawn, and the vicar's wife poured tea and
mixed condescension with the deference due to the brand-new master and mistress of Lady Grove. My uncle and the vicar, an Oxford
man, chatted; and the vicar observed that there were some remarkable people said to be socialists today. The English were too indivi-
dualistic for that silliness, said my uncle. A well-known playwright
among them, too, said the vicar . . . can't recollect his name, though.
We're pleased Lady Grove is occupied, said the vicar . . . the English village wants something without the influence of the great
house. My uncle puffed his cigar. The English countryside hmmm,
said my uncle, got to be shored-up, so to speak; should get some
cricket out here; have a May Queen; all this good for chaps; get light
railway, machinery, progress, capital, new methods, crisp ideas;
great new things to be done out in the villages, pickles, jams, home-
grown and packed in the country; yes, yes. There was a brief spasm
of dismay evident of the vicar's face.

Later in the afternoon my aunt broke her long silence. Just like that, he buys the place, and what a bundle of chores for me. and now I'm a fine lady, just when Chiselhurst had gotten homey. This will really be *home,* replied my uncle; we've gotten there, Susan, gotten there at last.

Lady Grove could hold the master of Tono-Bungay for just so long. The feeling of satisfied accomplishment rapidly gave way to visions of a greater house, something beyond the late medieval and Tudor confinement of the present residence. Crest Hill was to be next. Edward Ponderevo, indeed, a notable figure publicly. His name appeared often in the newspapers; he was honored by a Vanity Fair caricature, and the New Gallery displayed a somewhat portly image of my uncle on one of Ewart's medallions.

As for myself, my scientific experiments had provided me with some reputation, and, irony of ironies, one person who sought to improve by association with me was Archie Garvell. He was a penniless soldier now and was forever making me privy to the infalliable instincts of his sporting blood. Of course, he had no recollection of our childhood encounter.

My uncle was at the height of his activity during those days. The machinery of his enterprises turned and seemed to reproduce itself incessantly. He was a commercial success, a captain of industry, but in some ways he had never changed—the Zzzz, the absent-minded fiddle with his glasses, and that rocking back on his heels at the end of some statement. They were, I recollect, the self-same mannerisms that were his when my mother had brought me to his Wimblehurst chemist shop to discuss my future. My uncle's vision was always on the summit of success. He was always erratic and excitable to romantic dreams of commercial grandeur. They stimulated him, made him almost giddy as his mind wandered over visions of getting things "afloat." The truth of the matter is that he never really had that much head to lose. Great wealth and power merely provided greater latitude for the wide swings of his imagination. There were times, though, when my uncle and I would talk. We talked once in June, up on Crest Hill where I had the sheds for my airplanes and balloons—Lady Grove lay below us. I told you, George, he said. We got there; Tono-Bungay did it. A great world. I hope those beggars back in Wimblehurst know that I'm the one that did it. Zzzz . . . millions of people, George . . . Zzzz . . . each doing. Whitman knew; he said it, whatever it was . . . but us . . . picked out . . . power, leisure . . . opportunities . . . grabbed them . . . held them . . . big people, growing people . . . great world, George, great world, Zzzz. And my uncle dreamed of a title, too. After all, people had gotten them who had done less. It's not, he said, like some scientific fellow who can't even earn a living. *That* was, I must admit, a sore point with us, and we'd rubbed together on it before.

Edward Ponderevo had his heroes, too. The superman concept of Nietzsche and the glorious image of Napoleon had the strongest appeal for him. He collected Napoleonic memorabilia to be sure, preferring those portraits that allowed a somewhat plumper dimension to the little emperor. I often feel that my uncle's collapse would have been less thunderous had not the romantic specter of Bonapart walked beside him during those final years.

Edward Ponderevo even had his fling at infidelity. I felt for aunt Susan, afraid of humiliation for her. But she surprised me. Passion is passion and all that, George, she said; but I won't let him make an old fool of himself. A lover, indeed, at his age. I'll mark every piece of his underwear, I will—*private*. Whatever transpired in the next few days, it brought my uncle up short. Of course, their relationship suffered for it; the ironic banter between them waned—Teddy Ponderevo's sparing imagination had been tethered for a bit. It was a splendid victory for Aunt Susan. There were, moreover, many victories for her at Lady Grove. The servants loved her, and she became masterful at jams and domestic wines. I might add, too, that my scientific work cost me financially—and I might well have devoted more attention to my uncle's enterprises. Great wealth drugged him. He spent and spent; he had no limit, and he recognized none. I do not believe that he wanted to face the facts; his buying became a fever. Crest Hill was to be Olympus. Galleries were to be here—galleries were to be there, and also an architect from the Royal Academy—specialist in landscape gardening—woodcarving—masonry—interior designer—workers in metal—engineers—scribes—painters—professionals of every stripe—of every enthusiasm. Edward Ponderevo was, after all, a symbol of his age. It was to be a palace—but how irrelevant, how totally inconsequential! I should say also that even a year after much of it had been erected, there was a disintegration, a shoddiness of workmanship, a dishonesty in the construction that made itself known. He had wanted a wall—eleven miles of it, too—but within a year, it had revealed what shabby disinterest was invested in its construction. Edward Ponderevo's dream was cheaply assembled.

I was still experimenting with my gliders and airships, and I chanced to spend some time in conversation with the vicar. "Incredible," he said — the look of the whole valley is changed. Temporary sacrileges, I replied, just temporary. I could understand his dismay.

CHAPTER III
Soaring

While my uncle was postulating Crest Hill, I had been engaged in the valley nearby with my aerial experiments. I worked on explosive engines, flight stability, the steering of inflated bags — and I also built more expansive facilities, carried away, I imagine, by some of my uncle's own extravagance. I then discovered Cothope, a working engineer of superb capacities and a grand assistant. Of course, I had the great satisfaction of being able to research without financial worries. I have discovered also that science is the only true reality in this life of ours. She is never perverse, never cheats, cannot be altered or cheapened by human promotions or enterprises. In my Wimblehurst days I had a natural inclination toward discipline, something that was displaced with the advent of London, Tono-Bungay, and wealth. My experiments with gliders set that right. My first glider, patterned somewhat on the ideas of the Wright brothers, flew successfully, and with that success I began to see a need of physical and mental discipline for myself. I abstained from smoking and drinking, ate carefully, and exercised often — sometimes in dangerous ways as a conditioning for flights yet to be made. It was good preparation for I did have smashups, and a broken rib, too.

It was one day while my uncle and I were walking back from a visit to the construction at Crest Hill that I encountered the Honorable Beatrice Normandy once again. She was riding with Archie Garvell and the old Earl of Carnaby. It was just as the Earl and my uncle had finished chatting that she finally recognized me, but she rode off with the others without saying a word. I had not recollected that Beatrice was the step-daughter of Lady Osprey, who lived nearby. It was twenty years since we played together at Bladesover, and now she was filling my thoughts once again. Lady Osprey and Beatrice then made an appointment to call and appeared a week later precisely at the announced time. Lady Osprey, plump and aristocratic, was given a tour of the house by my aunt, who, I am certain, struck this lady of quality as most eccentric in speech and gesture. Beatrice allowed Lady Osprey and my aunt to outdistance us on the tour, and so we were able to talk. All this, she said, referring to the house — how did it all happen for you? Things *have* happened, I replied. My uncle is now a great man of finance, and we're part of the new breed — promoters — doers.

Afterwards, Beatrice was always on my mind; but I did work well at my experiments, and in the spring I got some short unstable runs out of a flying machine. It was from these experiments that I wrote several papers, eventually leading to my designation as Fellow of the Royal Society. I then began fitting a gas bag and glider together in an effort at increased navigability. This first such machine I called the Lord Roberts Alpha at my uncle's request. There was much notoriety to be derived from what was now becoming a rather competitive field, and my uncle was most agreeable to investing in my experiments. The Lord Roberts Alpha, however, crashed. It was engine-powered but had a gas bag that could be netted in. Once the machine was sufficiently aloft, the gas bag could be retracted, so to speak; and the result would be a truly heavier-than-air craft. But the Lord Roberts Alpha crashed into a grove of trees, and the side of my face was severely injured. I had attempted to walk away from the crash and had collapsed. Cothope was first at the scene, quickly followed by Beatrice and Lord Carnaby, who had been out riding. In her haste to get to me, Beatrice had even fallen from her horse. She was determined, Cothope told me later, that she should be the one to nurse and restore me to health. The crash had occurred in October; but between June when I met her and then, our relationship had intensified and deepened. She made no effort to conceal her interest in me, and I imagine that I did love her; it was, I think, romantic love. It was not the yearning I had for Marion or the purely sensual response as there was with Effie Rink — it was different somehow, and it elicited the adolescent in me; that I know. I was keenly interested in the effect my words and actions would have upon her. I dreamed of wonderful situations and I wanted to do superb things, brave things. It could be said that I acted with Beatrice in mind as an audience and with myself on stage. But there were moments when my romantic dreaming was replaced by passion; and so, when I had crashed and been taken under Beatrice's care to her stepmother's house at Bedley Corner, I lay there wrapped in bandages and I asked her to marry me. No, she said, no; it is impossible. It can never be, never. But what is, I said . . . why? . . . my social position? No, she replied, but it could never be; she could never marry me. Through it all, there was something she wanted to say, something she wanted to explain, but could not. When she had left the room, I was frustrated and angered, and I left my bed and tried clumsily to dress. With the arrival of the nurse, I demanded to see Beatrice again, the only condition upon which I would return to bed. When she came to me her mood had changed. Inconsiderate and willful were the words she used to describe herself. Forgive me . . . yes, of course I shall marry you . . . women are such victims of mood and whim. I asked her why she had said no. There are some obstacles

. . . problems . . . but we shall talk of them when you are well, she said. I was happy now, and I closed my eyes. I did not care what complications there might be.

After I returned to Lady Grove, Beatrice called once, bringing flowers and announcing that she was to spend some time in London. My aunt Susan had little to say, but she had watched my relationship with Beatrice, had watched it cautiously and somewhat fearfully. Even after Beatrice returned from London, she never managed to see me alone—or without Carnaby. Gradually Carnaby emerged from the background to stand before me significantly as a rival, someone who had a grip upon Beatrice, a claim of some kind. But there were other things in the works as well. I had formulated plans for the Lord Roberts B even before the bandages were removed. It was to be much larger than the Lord Roberts A and would capably carry two or three men. Then, too, some of my uncle's promotions had become suspect. Public doubt began to crop up where there had never been doubt before. The great pyramid of credit was trembling. Eventually, Beatrice and I bickered about Carnaby, and in retrospect I see that my conduct was unworthy. I was much less than the man I should have been.

CHAPTER IV
How I Stole the Heaps of Quap from Mordet Island

I decided to go up to London, to the Hardingham Hotel, to learn just what state things were in with my uncle's finances. We have a fight on our hands, was his reply; we're going to have to face up to things. It's Lord Boom and his damn newspapers, too, he added. Down on me, got a scare going, reporters hanging about; we're solid though, solid; damn Boom, making money tight for us. Why not trim expenses, I said, stop work on Crest Hill for a while. Never, he broke in, never. I'll never stop Crest Hill for Boom. Besides it would be too obvious. No, must continue with Crest Hill right to the end. But that quap, George, that quap. There's great value there. And it's got canadium, just what's needed for the perfect filament. With the quap, we'll be saved, George, and we'll give Boom what he deserves, too. Gordon-Nasmyth was to leave on Tuesday in a brig to get the quap from Mordet Island. A brig? I said. There are two gunboats down there; it's international grand theft, and you send him off in a brig. It should have been a steamer. I should have been into this thing long ago, I said. My uncle opened a telegram that had been lying on his desk. His face whitened. It's Nasmyth, an auto accident; he can't go for the quap. All right, I said rather declaratively; I'll go. I'll get it.

From Gordon-Nasmyth in his hopital bed I got all the information I could, and with Pollack, his cousin, I went down to Gravesend to see our ship, the *Maud Mary*. The vessel was a sorry object to behold, more accustomed to carrying potatoes. The captain, a Rumanian Jew, believed that we were to go after copper ore. The crew, on the whole, matched the condition of the ship. Two days were spent preparing the vessel, and then I returned to see Beatrice and tell her of the voyage. Lady Osprey, pink and plump, put a damper on our conversation, and Beatrice whispered that I should meet her at midnight by the garden wall. At the appointed time she was there, and we walked along the lane together and into the Old Woking Road in the cold rain of that January night. We walked and she wanted us to pretend we were not alive; out of life, she said, out of the complications and the judgments of this stupid world. Don't speak, she said, no explanations now. I want it this way, as though we weren't part of the world any more. I'm confused, I replied, about your marrying me. . . . I thought—don't speak, she said, let me speak for us. And for the remainder of our walk on that rainy night, she spoke of love with such beauty, such joy and tender understanding that I scarcely know how to describe it. At the gate in the wall, she paused and assured me that she would await my return. I love you, she said, I love you *now*. In a moment I was alone in the drizzle and the night, brought out of my dreaming. The door was shut, and Beatrice was gone.

The venture aboard the *Maud Mary* to Mordet Island was not the sort that makes for satisfying memories. The weather was foul, and I became seasick for the only time in my life. On the return voyage everyone became ill, and no doubt it was due to being poisoned by the quap. I was quartered with Pollack and the captain, and a more tedious pair of individuals would be difficult to discover. Pollack was very dramatically seasick, and at other moments smoked his pipe, which blended rather unfortunately with the ship's native aroma of potatoes. The captain, for his part, was most curious about our journey and had a strong bias against things English. No aristocracy in England, he would say, only middle class and profits, no art, no philosophy, only profit and get rich. He was obsessively anti-British, a slovenly captain, and a man for whom the Bible-reading mate had only one word of contempt—Dago. Up forward, the rest of the crew lived much as we did on this slum of a ship—cramped, filthy, roach-infested. These old sailing ships make good stuff for romantic reading; but after fifty-three days out, the romance is dead. This African adventure was a thing by itself, and for a time it drove thoughts of Beatrice, my uncle and my soaring experiments from my mind. Once at Mordet Island, the captain became balky about stealing the quap, and his ethical balance could only be righted by an offer of a ten per cent commission for the extraordinary risks he was assuming.

I am certain that the quap we removed was only a fraction of a massive deposit that sloped down and seaward. But the infectious quality of the stuff was something with which to be reckoned; it was radioactive, catching hold and spreading, eating and decaying. What if a man and his world were to end in this manner, I wondered? What if there were no glorious finale to man's efforts — only atomic disintegration? Such a belief, however, would make life purposeless; but the possibility exists. Science and reason do not rule it out.

At Mordet Island, the weather was generally oppressive with heat, fog and rain. Wheelbarrow after wheelbarrow of quap was run up the plankway and dumped into the hold, and with each load my apprehension about discovery increased. It had become impossible for me to sleep. I was extremely irritable and restless, and took to long walks in the mornings. On one of these, I came face to face with a native, a squat black fellow. He started and I stared, and then he ran. I cried out in English for him to stop, but he ran with great agility over the roots and twisted vines that lay everywhere. No, no, I thought, he'll tell, he can't get away, and so I raised my gun and fired. He fell, struck between the shoulder blades, and was dead. It was murder, an unreasonable act, but I recollect, too, a sense of swift elation as I fired and the bullet brought the fleeing creature down in an instant. I had murdered a man. I was unable to forget him, though, and twice I returned to the spot where I had pushed his dead body beneath the soft mud with my rifle butt. On the second occasion, he was gone, and there were human footprints about.

We all had enough of the place, both the crew and I, and as it turned out, we were none too soon in getting the ship homeward bound. Our presence was known, and it was only through luck and the cover of heavy mists that the *Maud Mary* was able to elude a gunboat that accosted us off the coast. Once at sea, I was relaxed and elated, even though the quap had made me ill. But then, of course, the ship began to break up. It was, I am certain, the effects of the radiation from the quap upon the wooden hull. We pumped and pumped, but the water seemed to flow in right through the planks.

During one of my turns at the futile pumping, Pollack came to me and announced that the captain says she's going down right now. And down the *Maud Mary* went while we watched from a longboat in which we had pulled clear of the hulk. We were picked up later by the *Portland Castle*, and it was only when I was back in London that I learned from the newspapers just how sweeping my uncle's bankruptcy had been.

COMMENT: In Book III Teddy Ponderevo ascends to even greater wealth, but his financial house of cards is trembling. A companion to this ascendency is his effort to rise socially. He develops the acquisitive tastes of the elegant, and he spends money without reason or restraint. There is the move from Beckenham to the Chiselhurst mansion, then on to Lady Grove—and then the reach for the sublime folly, Crest Hill, grotesque, sprawling, and shoddily built. It is the symbol of Edward Ponderevo's loss of balanced control over the enterprises of Tono-Bungay, but more significantly over himself. He has become giddy with enterprise, giddy with wealth and power. His financial giant, once ruled with an intuitive genius, now rules him, and in its waywardness is about to crush its creator. And through the pathetic folly of this little man now driven headlong toward disaster is the figure of Aunt Susan, unpretentious, warmly human and loveable, loving Teddy Ponderevo no differently at that moment than she did when they occupied the little chemist shop in Wimblehurst. How patient she is with this often silly man, who has grown beyond his capacity to grow.

For George Ponderevo there is the reintroduction of Beatrice Normandy, now enigmatic and perplexing in her profession of love for him and in the tormented and mysterious way she handles his proposal. It is interesting to note that George Ponderevo is guilty of some exhibitionism in his relationship with Beatrice. He wants to do great things for her, and this conduct is not unlike the boyish dreams of success he entertained in their childhood days at Bladesover. But Beatrice, Edward Ponderevo and Crest Hill are forgotten on the wild journey to the African coast to steal the mounds of quap. The Ponderevos have an option on a filament for electric lamps, and in the radioactive quap is a valuable substance essential for the filament. A successful capture of the quap will return Edward Ponderevo's tottering empire to solvency. Failure would mean disaster for the colossus that sprang from the exhilarating Tono-Bungay.

The pursuit of the quap is episodic, indeed, presenting itself as a separate frame in the overall tapestry of Book III and the novel itself. It is an adventure in which Wells makes a curious commentary on human nature. George Ponderevo kills a man, and he is astounded not simply by the act itself, but by the ease and matter-of-fact attitude with which he does it and disposes of the body. It is with "a leap of pure exaltation" that he pulls the trigger and slays the running native with one well-placed shot. For a moment George's background and training are forgotten. Quite cooly, and without passion of any sort, he destroys a fellow human being. Interestingly enough, the scientist in George never quite quits him as he recounts with scientific objectivity his actions and responses to the killing. It should be noted also that Wells does not moralize here. There is no overriding sense of moral guilt for George, even though his dreams are made nightmarish by visions of the dead savage. If we felt that Wells had overdone George Ponderevo's sense of mental and moral superiority over his uncle, who is always tainted with shallowness and blantant fraud in the novel, this act seems to return him, at least for the moment, to human fallibility. But George Ponderevo's murder of the native appears to be chalked up to expediency and quap sickness by Wells more than to character weakness. Actually Wells never allows George Ponderevo to become as frail and deranged as the little promoter with the Napoleon fixation. Wells assigns the murder with about equal value to the episodic scheme that he has created. Taken within the context of the entire novel, it assumes the character of an extreme act, nothing more, one of the colorful highs on the chart of George Ponderevo's experiences.

BOOK THE FOURTH
The Aftermath of Tono-Bungay

CHAPTER I
The Stick of the Rocket

At the Hardingham Hotel, I told my uncle that the quap was gone, sunk to the floor of the Atlantic. They've been at me for a week, he said, nipping at me on all sides. He filled a small glass with some medicine from one of several bottles on his cluttered desk. Sour luck, George, sour, get out of it, down to Crest Hill. The medicine had an aroma, and it was strangely familiar. Stomach, George, he said, been acting up, you know. But Napoleon did it, Russia, even Waterloo . . . stomach, even worse than mine. He reached for more of the medicine, and his spirits quickened, his confidence returned. At battle, George, he said, but I'm not done yet . . . cards to be played before we're through, yes, sir, cards to be played. I'll be down to Lady Grove tomorrow, George. Oh Lord! Thanks for weekends.

At Lady Grove I saw my aunt Susan. I had wanted to help, she confessed, but he and I never had the same way of doing things. Wealth made us approach things differently. I just don't know what's up, and I can't really get near him. I'm always in the dark, you know. The servants are always getting the nastiest of the papers out of sight. Poor, poor Teddy, up to his ears in it, I imagine. Hard on him, very hard, I know.

It was a sweetly splendid May, and after breakfast I made my way up to the sheds at Crest Hill to see what Cothope was about with the Lord Roberts B. Terrible, sir, said Cothope; it's all coming down around us. A great shame. All this work should be free of that sort of thing, supported by the state, if you'll pardon me sir. Right, I said, I've always had a touch of the socialist in my blood; I understand what you mean. We examined the Lord Roberts B, and Cothope expanded somewhat. It's good to know you're a socialist, sir, he said. I'm one and have been one for quite a while . . . only thing. A cutthroat business this world is, everyone tumbling over one another. The scientific people like ourselves will just have to take things in hand, get all this promotion and puffy advertising out of the picture. Just look what it's done to us now.

Cothope and I worked on the Lord Roberts B all that morning, filling the gas bag and making adjustments wherever necessary. I thought of Beatrice then, and I longed for her. At Bedley Corner both she and Lady Osprey were out, and so I walked along the lane towards Woking, along the path we had taken together five months before. I passed by the grotesque presumption of the Crest Hill construction, and it gave me to thinking. This was the product of all our efforts. The enterprises of Teddy Ponderevo had come to this. It was the style of our age. But was it life . . . was it really living? Is this what society and its struggles are all about?

Then suddenly, I met my uncle, and there were tears in his eyes. Oh, how they had badgered him, pressed him, had all their ammunition ready, making a man contradict himself. . . and Neal . . . after all I'd done for Neal, pressing me, ready to ruin me. It's like Russia, George. He was ashamed; I could see that, and it pained me deeply to see my uncle gaze so pathetically at the never-to-be-completed work at Crest Hill. I formed a plan. It was bold, but it might work. We would cross the Channel in the Lord Roberts B. Once in Brittany or Normandy, we would materialize as tourists. After all, he was soon to be a pursued man, and this appeared to be the only way out of it. My aunt was a match for the situation as I knew she would be. Forgery, I said to her, I think it's forgery he's been up to. It's going to be a tight one, I added; you must do what you can, get together what you can, and follow us. Oh, I wish I could help him, George, she said; my Teddy, little Teddy; poor, poor Teddy.

I did get my uncle on the Lord Roberts B, and our flight was launched across the Surrey and Sussex countryside. In the night I must have dozed, having shut off the engine and allowing the machine to drift. But the wind shifted, we went off course and far down Channel. In the darkness, my uncle chattered to himself, eagerly and to an imaginary audience. I did see lights from Bordeaux, but it was some fifty miles from there that we finally dropped. When we set down, my uncle and I tumbled out; and the ship seemed to have a will of its own and to want to be up and off for itself. One of the ropes slipped away from me and I pursued it, but it got too far ahead. The Lord Roberts B was free and untethered, and I watched it recede up and into the horizon. It was never discovered, and I believe that was much the best thing.

My uncle sat chilled. He munched some biscuits, finished what remained in our flasks. His face was flushed, perhaps feverish, and the gray stubble on his chin granted him an appearance of age I was not accustomed to seeing. It was dawn and not a time to appear at some inn wearied and wanting rest. It would be too obvious. We would have to wait until later in the day, when our appearance would lead people to believe that we had spent some time on the road. He complained a bit. Not young any more, he said. He wept some and finally slept. I was tired, too, and I think I dozed.

Later in the day, we discovered an inn maintained by a gentle Basque woman. By that time I was convinced that my uncle was ill and growing worse. On the following morning, we obtainted a doctor. Cold . . . exposure, he said, pneumonia, too. I engaged a religious to attend my uncle and took a room at an inn nearby. The succeeding days blur for me, and I do not remember clearly the comings and goings of people in my uncle's room. However, my own impressions of him are clearly in my mind. He knew full well that he was dying, and there were some remarkable periods of clarity during his delirium. His mind ran to visions of grandeur and self-approval. A great residence, he remarked, terraces. Upward, going upward . . . house of a financial giant. Zzzz, millions. Zzzz, commerce.

Gradually, public suspicion grew about the small dying man in the curtained bed. Strange faces appeared at the inn, the newspapers were getting hot, and we were now regarded as something more than middle-class tourists who had unhappily been overtaken by sickness. Then, without warning, we were set upon by an Anglican clergyman, suspecting my uncle's identity and profoundly impressed by his notorious financial stature. He bubbled over and he was busily attentive. And then in the middle of the night, he rapped on my door telling me I must come at once if I wished to see my uncle alive. There was even the Basque landlady who tried to force a crucifix on my uncle. The religious hovered about; and there were other people there, committed it seems, to be present at the final life's breath. But my uncle was not on schedule. He did not die then. It was a matter of another night until the end came. By that time I had hustled the clergyman out amid kneeling and fervid prayers, and did not allow him near my uncle again. My uncle, in one of his lucid moments, remarked on the clergyman and how he was after something, wanted something. It was only a momentary suspicion on my part that his attention to my uncle was grounded on other than spiritual motive, but I am certain that I was wrong. He was a simple man, honest and good, to be sure. Very near the time when he died, my uncle's mind cleared and we spoke. Do you think there is? he said. What? I answered. Something beyond, another world, some other world, he said. Perhaps? Perhaps? Yes, I replied, I'm just about certain of it. In a little while he died, slowly and calmly, and I did not even notice the moment of his passing.

Later I thought how unreal it all was, all the ambitions, the desires, the dreams. I felt as if I had died as well. When my aunt Susan came, it was too late; Teddy Ponderevo had died. Life is queer, she said, that I should ever have imagined all this to end this way. You, George, all grown and a man, and me just about an old woman. And Teddy, Teddy . . . that I should think . . . dear Teddy. And suddenly all the tears came, and it was good that they did. Oh, I wonder if they'll let him have his say in heaven . . . oh, George, it hurts so much. But he was like my own child that life abused, a foolish child, and I never had much say in the matter. Why couldn't they just let him be, George, just let him go his way?

CHAPTER II
Love Among the Wreckage

Upon my return to England, I discovered that my association with my uncle in flight from persecution had rendered me a sinisterly popular individual. Honesty, it seems, never appeals to the average man in the way that daring and the shadily adventuresome do. The receivers even permitted me two weeks to clean my notes and papers out of the Crest Hill sheds. As for Cothope, I placed him with the Ilchesters, the people for whom I now build warships. And then there was Beatrice, riding up on Carnaby's fine black horse to where I sat on the terrace at Lady Grove. I would like to see your cottage, she said, after a while, the place where you live. We went there and spoke of music; Beethoven, the Kreutzer Sonata and Brahms. We set a roll in the pianola, and it made the moment beautiful. How lovely, she said, it's so moving. Suddenly we were embracing, kissing, and all I could say was, Beatrice, Beatrice!

I took it all quite seriously then as though nothing else mattered in the world, but it was purposeless and futile, too. She told me about her girlhood years. She had not married; the opportunities had not seemed particularly promising. That was when Carnaby came along. You realize? she said. Yes, I replied. She told me that she did come very near marrying me, but she was unwilling to sink into ruin and poverty. I've been spoiled. I've been sold and bought. It was not a question, you see, of not being good enough for me. We are lovers, dear, she said; but think of those times when we are not lovers, the gulf, the distance between us, the ways we respond from training, our thoughts are different, our habits. We're each ruined in our own way.

I asked Beatrice to marry me once again, but this was to be our last time together. It was morning, very early, and the sun would not shine anywhere that day. Marry me, I had said to her, honestly. Bear me children. It's impossible, she responded. The world is the cause of what we are. It breeds every wrong inclination and response in us. Wealth can destroy a person as well as poverty can. We were silent for a while, but I thought I heard her say, "Chloral." It might have been my imagination, an unreal thought; but the word remains in my memory . . . chloral . . . a drug, you know. Our good-byes were quick, then, over and done with, and it was ended for us.

But I saw her again, riding with Carnaby, and her face turned white as she prodded her horse past me. Carnaby felt superior under my notorious circumstances and saluted me in a most gentlemanly way. The agony I felt did not pass with them, and the pain has remained, and still remains as I write this book. It hangs over me as an eternally dark shadow.

CHAPTER III
Night and the Open Sea

The story is told. But these manuscript pages before me have no meaning now, unless they reflect waste, sterility and an energy that bore only futility. I think of Marion and my aunt Susan, both childless; and I think of Beatrice, wasted without purpose. My thoughts turn about to Crest Hill and to commerce, to the struggle for more wealth, for more pleasure. It is late in the season, it seems to me, for this way of life. To others such affairs may represent progress. History alone will judge, but I discover little promise in our times and in our ways.

It was some three weeks ago that I paused in writing this book to devote necessary time and attention to final adjustments on the X2, the destroyer I have been building. Last week I took her through her paces down the Thames. And there, passing down the river, it was all England that seemed to be flooding before me. This was what I had wanted the book to be about. It was a panorama, and at its center was Parliament, busy and contending. It seemed to cry out for the respect, but I would not be the one to respond, not the one to honor its Bladesover ways. It's all there, the pomp and tinsel of respectability, and the dignity, too; but no one is deceived. Thus, to pass down the Thames is to touch the features of the English countenance itself. There is a landscape of industrialism, residences of kings and clergymen, ranges of squalid dwellings, Westminster Bridge, Georgean and Victorian architecture — and St. Paul's, austere symbol of old Anglicanism. Finally, there is the last movement in this symphony of London — London Bridge, introducing one to that mistress of change, the sea. The seaport itself, active, cluttered, masts and hulls and wharves pressed in thickly together, as if it were all haphazard, assembled without order or intention. Then there is the sea, and my destroyer and I are in the open with familiar lights and shapes of land falling behind — the memories, the old pride and devotions sink like London and England, behind and down beyond sight.

In this novel I have attempted to present England in its feudal structure, infected with a destructive flabbiness, with abnormal and puffy growth. There is a confusion here, too, a great bubbling stew of sounds and desires and actions. But there *is* something that swirls out of it, something that draws people like myself on. I can't define it, perhaps because it is too pure, too far beyond substance. It might be called Truth. It is, however, a reality I identify with science; but there are others who have found it in art, in music, in literature and in social innovation. It takes many forms for many men, and its appearance has as many shapes. At this moment, it is symbolized by my destroyer; elemental, starkly pure and wonderfully beautiful.

It was not until the following morning that my ship turned back to London, and those damp and famished newsmen, who accompanied me, were back on shore. As for the destroyer, it is not for England, and it is not for the nations of Europe. The X2 was offered to the English, but they wished no part of me. It matters little, though, for I have managed to develop a certain detachment, to observe myself and my nation from a distance, from the outside, so to speak, with the picture I see uncolored and undistorted. We all have our moments and then are gone each with his own purpose, each with his own destiny — out, as it were, into the vastness of the sea.

COMMENT: In this final section of the novel, Teddy Ponderevo dies, a pitiful figure, appearing smaller than life size in his last hours. For George Ponderevo, who is more Wells than anything else, Teddy Ponderevo is a product of the system that boosts the vulgarly fraudulent and commercially shabby to the heights of wealth and power. If Teddy was a commercial giant in life, Wells does not permit him a giant's death. It is a sniveling delirious thing, mixed with whimpers and doubts about the hereafter, and punctuated with inarticulate visions of scope and financial importance. There is, however, in George Ponderevo, a persistent and annoying sense of moral and ethical superiority. This is Wells, who never truly allows George to live a fictional life totally distinct from his creator. Wells is always there to step in with social judgment, with an acknowledgment of socialist theory, and a tisk-tisk for the system that can spawn a fraudulent entrepreneur and the pure scientist like himself.

If there is a time when George Ponderevo is more believable as a fictional character, it is during the Bladesover days and perhaps those of his young manhood as well. There is much that is autobiographically Wells here, but there is a fictional identity for George here, too. It is particularly in the last section of Book IV that Wells/Ponderevo forces himself above and beyond his characters. It is almost as if he has said: "I shall be better than those of whom I write." Edward Ponderevo is dead. The women George has known are childless and wasted. Beatrice, for whom there seemed to be some hope, in the end falls beneath the weight that an aristocratic social shallowness has pressed upon her.

It is true that Wells allows George Ponderevo some human frailty, but the final portion of Book IV brings George to philosophical and professional triumph, despite the system. Sailing his destroyer down the Thames and into the sea, he is alone, independent and self-sufficient.

Here, at the conclusion of the book, Wells, the social reformer and visionary, emerges to cry out that all England is shallow, aimless, confused and suffering from awkward and irrelevant growth. There was the antiquated crumbling of Bladesoverian ways, symbolized in the wrinkled and trembling Lady Drew, a system atrophied but perpetuated in its silly ignorant ritualism. Then there are the new people, important and clever little people like Teddy Ponderevo. Their rise is due, Wells says, as much to the accidents of a wayward capitalism and its top-heavy lust for wealth, power and pleasure as it is to the lovable little man's charlatan genius. In the final moments of the novel, all this seems to slip beneath the waves, and George Ponderevo is left with pure commitment. Science — truth — it is indefinable, but one follows it, and it emerges the one worthwhile thing for the great social and economic maelstrom that Wells believed his England to be.

CHARACTER ANALYSIS

GEORGE AND EDWARD PONDEREVO: It should be recognized immediately that H. G. Wells casts himself in the role of George Ponderevo, employing him as a vehicle for his criticism of life and society. George passes much of his boyhood at Bladesover, a great country house, where he has the opportunity to become increasingly aware of the shallowness of the aristocratic code and the woeful narrowness of class consciousness. From his Bladesover days, George enters the world with an ethical code to which he himself is not always faithful. His association with Tono-Bungay begins with the realization that essentially it is fraudulent and that its promotion must be fraudulent also. Yet, his desire to marry Marion Ramboat compromises his ethical position. In time, his elaborate and expensive experiments with airships come to depend upon the income from his uncle's promotions, even though George himself has little to do with the management of the tottering financial empire.

George Ponderevo's relationships with women prove ultimately to be unfulfilling. With an ignorantly adolescent romantic preparation for marriage, George finally wins Marion, an attractive but frigid young woman. During their relatively short married life, George is as blundering as Marion is terrified; and so the marriage is a failure, even from its courtship days. From Effie Rink, George receives the physical gratification absent in his marriage with Marion; but it is not until he encounters Beatrice Normandy, now a mature woman, that he truly falls in love. With her there is the promise of a full relationship, but their marriage is never to be. George's remark that he seemed destined to be an ineffectual lover is not entirely accurate; his failure to win Beatrice from her place as Lord Carnaby's mistress is much the fault of the ease and wealth to which she had become so accustomed that foresaking it would be impossible.

Almost from the beginning of the Tono-Bungay ascendency, George regards himself as a stronger and more intelligent person than his uncle Teddy. How then does Wells maintain this superiority in the face of Teddy's rise to fortune and power? He does so by maintaining George Ponderevo's basic ethical strength despite a partial compromise with Tono-Bungay wealth. In addition, George rises to fame and a fellowship in the Royal Academy through the purity and uncompromising honesty of science — not by means of the fraudulence of big business promotions. When crisis finally confronts George and Teddy Ponderevo, it is Teddy who breaks down, partly from illness, but also from an endemic weakness of nature — he is not a courageous man. It is George who maintains his composure and engineers the daring flight across the Channel with the whimpering Teddy in tow. At the conclusion of the book, George Ponderevo rises as nobly as science itself, uncontaminated by his adventures, a Wellsian construction standing in triumph over society and system.

Teddy Ponderevo, the little man of cleverness and Napoleonic delusions, is as much propelled to importance by the public's native gullibility and a ripeness for enterprising sham as he is by his own promotional genius. Wells is saying that without society's ethical softness and the economic disease of capitalistic big-money "flotations," Teddy would never have succeeded. He is a symbol of the newly rich commercial class. He has arrived, and he has displaced the ossified Lady Drews from their dynastic perches.

Teddy Ponderevo's road to a great fortune is paved with slick advertising and shoddy illusion, but he is given a respectable substance by lavish spending and splendid houses. However, the staggering symbols of his wealth only mask Edward Ponderevo's basic weaknesses. The success of his Tono-Bungay dream has led him hopelessly into a giddy upward movement in which one frail scheme teeters precariously upon the one beneath it. The momentum of his financial enterprises soon outdistances him, and his initial genius for promotional advertising gives way to a dizzy euphoria manifesting itself in the folly of a spreading and graceless Crest Hill.

If Teddy's capitalistic schemes revolt the socialist in Wells, his character is not treated unsympathetically altogether. He has a lovable quaintness about him; and even at the height of his wealth and power, he seems more like a child playing at maturity, a little boy dressed in a Napoleonic uniform and affecting, rather poorly, an imperial manner. Both George and Aunt Susan recognize Teddy's incapacities and limitations. They understand all too well that "the bitch-goddess success," as the psychologist William James termed it, has elevated him to an atmosphere far too rare for Teddy's survival. He is lovably weak amid the toys of his success, and we come to pity him as a fictional character and not reject him as a symbol of social and economic corruption. Wells never wished us to reject him as a character; after all, he was not creating Teddy as a villian. Wells does not allow him steely adamant for a heart and a totally ruthless engagement with the world. We could not be compassionate toward Teddy if we discovered these things in him. His weakness gives him a warmly realistic appeal; and as much as Wells appreciates the collapse of the preposterous Tono-Bungay success, he does not destroy Teddy's appeal with it. The socialist/novelist has not brought down his character with a double blow. The socialist triumphs, but so does the novelist by permitting a literary tenderness to temper the socialist's outrage. The death of Teddy Ponderevo is pitiful, but this is how the fraudulent giant must fall. There must be no tragic descent from grandeur. It is not a great man who is falling. The promotor, at once the victim and the instrument of the system, must diminish in stature considerably — but more accurately, he must reveal what he has always been basically. Wells tells us that the weak and shallow man, lovable and unwise, is tainted with the stain of commercial sordidness.

THE WOMEN OF *TONO-BUNGAY*:   None of the women in *Tono-Bungay* are destined for complete happiness. There is a futility and lack of personal realization for each of them. Marion Ramboat is fearful of the physical side of marriage and frigid when she finally meets it. She is inhibited and repressed by the sexual ignorance that society has thrust upon her, and she is a hopeless marriage partner for George Ponderevo. Marion Ramboat is not an intelligent girl. She lacks spirit and imagination as well, and her personality is a prosaic thing at best. She is physically attractive, and this is the basis of her appeal for George.

Effie Rink is no more than a sensual interlude for George Ponderevo. Her appeal is chemical, and she provides George with the physical satisfactions unattainable in his marriage to Marion.

Beatrice Normandy offers the only ideal womanly balance that George encounters. She is lovely, responsive and intelligent. In her George Ponderevo might discover a truly compatible mate. However, Beatrice Normandy is as bound to the responses of her class as Marion Ramboat was to those of her own lower-middle level. Marion's responses to life were dull, without range and limited by the low horizons of her class. She would always be what society and her social level had made her. Beatrice Normandy is really no different in this respect. An exciting young woman, she has been destroyed by the tastes that her aristocratic circles had cultivated in her. She could never live without wealth and is willing to sacrifice her honor in order to maintain her way of life. However, she is sufficiently intelligent and candid to recognize this weakness; and she readily confesses it to George.

Without question Aunt Susan is the most charming of all Wells's female characters in the novel. The critic Montgomery Belgion has remarked that she is a mere "shadow" with a vitality dependent upon the presence of George Ponderevo. The observation does a disservice to the loveliest character in the book, one of the most fully realized characters in Wells's literary art. It is interesting to contrast Susan's steady unaltered values with her husband's soaring frivolity. She is the stronger of the two and recognizes his instability all too well. She loves him and yet regards him as a child who requires understanding and patience. In George Ponderevo, she finds the son that she and Teddy never had; and in Aunt Susan George discovers the motherly affection and tenderness that he never received from his own mother.

None of the women in *Tono-Bungay* ever truly escaped the boundary lines of their social class. Aunt Susan is older but no different in the midst of wealth than she was in the early days at the chemist's shop in Wimblehurst. Marion is wrapped so suffocatingly in the restrictions and colorless horizons of her environment that her personality and desires are crippled from the beginning. Beatrice Normandy is held fast by the standards of her aristocratic class, and even the love of George Ponderevo cannot break their grasp upon her. George's mother, of all women in the book, is most fearfully aware of her place in the social order. Resignation to one's place and a proper awareness of the greater and lesser positions of others was for her an important lesson to teach her son. "Poor, proud, habitual, sternly narrow soul!" cries George in recalling his mother. For her, innovation would have been impossible.

None of the *Tono-Bungay* women discover a real fulfillment in life. George's father had left his mother, and she was left alone to raise a son who reminded her so much of the man. Aunt Susan, instinctively maternal, is without children of her own. Marion's marriage to George is totally unrewarding and childless. Effie Rink's future with some insignificant poet does not appear to offer an ultimate fulfillment. Beatrice Normandy is a wasted woman, as in some ways are all the women Wells has created in *Tono-Bungay*.

TEST QUESTIONS

1. Is it fair to say that Wells used fiction as a vehicle for social criticism? Justify your opinion with references to at least four of Wells's novels.

ANSWER: Certainly it is fair to characterize Wells as a social critic even in his fiction. Of the four novels that I shall refer to, *Tono-Bungay* contains the strongest social criticism. In *Tono-Bungay*, Wells actually points a finger in several directions. He condemns the lock-step social hierarchy represented by Bladesover, an aristocratic stiffness of shallow values and delicate sensibilities. For Wells, it was a dying system, a condemnable feudalism that would be replaced. But what about the values of the new class that would move into the Bladesovers and similar estates when the Lady Drews of English society were dead? It is this new commercial class that is assuming power in *Tono-Bungay*. The Teddy Ponderevos, top-heavy with wealth and importance, capitalizing upon fraudulent advertising and clever promotions, are as reprehensible in their exploitation and tasteless expansiveness as were the Bladesover gentry in their priggish intolerance.

For Wells, however, there is a strange parallel between the evolution of society toward a better world and the advances of pure science. At the conclusion of *Tono-Bungay*, George Ponderevo speaks of a certain indefinable "something" that draws some men on. Some, he says, discover it in art, others in literature, others in "social innovation." For him it is science and a truth he identifies there; a faithful thing, unbent by the perverse winds of social and economic change.

Herbert George Wells was also a critic of educational practices. His own early instruction and his belief in a broader, more rounded education led him to score educational deficiencies wherever he could. George Ponderevo is compelled to read the best books secretly at Bladesover and is told by his mother to learn Latin at his uncle's, not because he wishes to, but because he is obliged to. Later, George complains that his scientific textbooks were limited and inadequate.

The ignorant repressiveness of Victorian sex education also came under assault from Wells. George Ponderevo has the misfortune to marry Marion Ramboat, frigid, inhibited and terrified by the idea of sex. Their marriage, then, is a failure; but George confesses that his own sexual education was so wanting that he brought as much ignorance to the marriage as did Marion.

Never Marxist, Wells is socialistic in his outlook; and the system of capitalism is permitted to reveal an abundance of abuses in the economic opportunities it provides. He became disenchanted with the Fabians and sought stronger and more direct solutions to problems he detected in society. The poor remained poor and painfully ignorant, for education was not for everyone. Housing conditions deteriorated rather than improved, and a person was locked mentally as well as actually into his class. But Wells is a utopian, too; the millennium is always somewhere beyond, like the very thing George Ponderevo pursues in science – distant, pure and almost indefinable. In the "scientific romances," Wells engages in social criticism, too. In *The Time Machine*, the Traveller speculates periodically on the possible paths civilization may have taken to produce the Upperworld Eloi and Under-world Morlocks. In *The Invisible Man*, Dr. Kemp gazes from his study window and meditates on possible social conditions in the future. In *The War of the Worlds*, the narrator advises us to think how we treat some of our fellow human beings before we condemn the Martians for their atrocities. He confesses to being a speculative philosopher and mentions that he had been writing some papers on moral ideas and the civilizing process when the Martians first attacked.

It is possible to become deeply absorbed in Wells's narratives; his story-telling power is strong. However, it is never possible to avoid completely his own particular social and moral admonitions. He punctures certitudes and convictions, the established Victorian certainties of religion, society and morals. Wells is part of a generation moving out of Victorian positiveness and into the social challenge of the twentieth century.

2. What is the significance of Wells's "scientific romances" today?

ANSWER: Wells's scientific romances are always good tales. Their excitement and narrative staying power cannot be denied. In their own day they were for the most part wildly imaginative, and their giddy scientific speculations were dazzling. Today, however, much of Wells's outlandishly fictionalized science can no longer be considered as such. Airplanes today fly faster than the speed of sound. Space, if not time, travel is already at hand. The laser is a likely outgrowth of Wells's Heat Ray. Construction and handling machines, now being developed for use on other planets, seem to hark back to the type used by the Martians in their work about the pits. The suffocating Black Smoke that the Martians spread across the countryside has many of the characteristics of poison gas warfare used in Europe in World War I. Anyone reading Wells's scientific romances today must continually remind himself that they were written on the threshold of the twentieth century. The temptation to contemporize them in every way is often quite powerful. Scientifically, Wells's imagination was disturbingly prophetic. Even in *Tono-Bungay*, Wells, as George Ponderevo, contemplates the radioactive quap and wonders if atomic decay is to be the fate of all man's efforts.

3. What were Wells's views about the function of the novel?

ANSWER: In 1911 Wells published his essay "The Contemporary Novel," which appeared in November in *The Fortnightly Review*. In the essay Wells was quick to register his disapproval of the notion that novels were nothing more than pleasurable diversion, charming little excursions for idle hours. Pretensions at established or traditional forms in the novel became invalid for Wells. It should be broad. It should be flexible. It should examine life, the human condition and the human conduct therein. The novel should be a "social mediator . . . the criticism of laws and institutions and of social dogmas and ideas . . . the seed of fruitful self-questioning." In *Tono-Bungay* George Ponderevo remarks: "My ideas of a novel all through are comprehensive rather than austere. . . ." Wells believed that the novel, in its elasticity, should be able to comprehend all facets of life: the political, the social, the financial and whatever else in human affairs might be vulnerable to the thrust of close examination.

4. To what extent is Wells's fiction autobiographical?

ANSWER: Wells's science fiction draws heavily on his own experience as a student of science and of the moral and social condition of mankind. However, in *Tono-Bungay*, we can look to even more recognizable fragments of Wells's own background. Before she married, Wells's mother had been a lady's maid employed at

Up Park, a great house in Hampshire. Later, she became house-keeper there. In 1881 Wells had been a chemist's assistant in Midhurst. In 1883, he broke with his position as a draper's apprentice in Southsea, and on a summer day walked seventeen miles toward Up Park to encounter his mother returning from Sunday church. A recollection of the early portions of *Tono-Bungay* will clearly reveal the introduction of such autobiographical material by Wells. The chemist's shop is present in the form of Uncle Teddy's pharmacy at Wimblehurst where George Ponderevo is an apprentice. The flight from the Frapps on a Sunday and the long walk to Bladesover to meet his mother returning from church discover real life counterparts in Wells's seventeen mile walk from his drapery apprenticeship to intercept his own mother. Wells's unhappy marriage to his cousin and her insistence on a long engagement parallels George Ponderevo's marriage to Marion Ramboat. In addition, the novel bristles with social and scientific commentary, a natural outgrowth of Wells's socialist bias and his training as a scientist. More arresting even than Wellsian autobiography in *Tono-Bungay* is the presence of Wells himself. George Ponderevo seems less a believable fictional character than he does a stand-in for the voice and presence of Herbert George Wells. There are even moments when Wells appears as Teddy Ponderevo. But even this is not unusual for Wells; in *The Time Machine*, he appears as both the narrator and Time Traveller himself. This type of living presence by an author is more than autobiographical. The author who wishes to be autobiographical will draw upon personal history and experience and accommodate it to his characters. Wells does this, to be sure; but more than this, he presents himself to his readers in the very thinly disguised *personae* of his leading characters.

5. What overall assessment can be made of Wells as a writer?

ANSWER: When the name of H. G. Wells is mentioned, most people immediately associate it with several examples of the finest science fiction ever written. Certainly the value of Wells's scientific romances cannot be denied; his vivid imagination was very often astoundingly prophetic. Today space travel alone — in Wells's day fantastic and visionary — is a reality. Travel through time is not a reality; however, Albert Einstein's theoretical work with a time-space continuum has brought the Time Traveller's journey within our imaginative reach. As a social commentator, Wells was not a great thinker. Some of his critical observations on society are not without merit, for hypocrisy of all sorts aggravated him. In his emphasis upon doom as the future of a wayward society, Wells might even be termed an anti-utopian, yet one hopeful of a socialist deliverance. However, in his later years, his influence waned considerably; his assaults on the establishment were more vituperation than practical solution. He was a highly imaginative writer and a social visionary, but he cannot be considered a great philosophical thinker. Above and beyond his scientific imagination and social vision, Wells is a literary figure of substantial proportion. In his powers of description and dramatization and in his bent towards social criticism, Wells has been accurately likened to Charles Dickens. Beyond this flattering comparison, Wells stands in his own right as a splendid writer, endowed with great narrative powers, a literary eye and ear to be envied, and the ability repeatedly to make the improbable seem more than possible. It will become apparent to even the casual reader of Wells that there are those moments in his prose when finer writing could not be imagined.

CRITICAL ESTIMATES OF H. G. WELLS

A. C. Ward: "Philosophically considered, [Wells] was no thinker: he was an imaginative artist gone astray. His great gifts of fantasy and humour enriched literature, but when in relation to practical politics his fancies seemed a mirage, humour deserted him and he was left embittered and spiritually bankrupt."

Montgomery Belgion: "The essential merit of Wells is, indeed, to have been thoroughly the child of his time. If we say of him . . . that his constructive criticism is impudent and only his destructive criticism any good — we have summed up the reasons why. . . . Wells the Sage [should] be helped in every way to endure."

Arthur C. Clarke: "Wells saw as clearly as anyone into the secret places of the heart, but he also saw the universe, with all its infinite promise and peril. He believed — though not blindly — that men were capable of improvement and might someday build sane and peaceful societies on all the worlds that lay within their reach."

Mark Hillegas: "Surely the single most spectacular manifestation of [a sense of detachment in] the Wellsian imagination is its preoccupation with the future. . . . Naturally the Wellsian imagination is drawn to certain characteristic subjects. It is fascinated by the revelations of man's place in time and space given to us by science, fascinated by the vistas of astronomy, particularly the death of the world and the vastness of interstellar space, fascinated by the vision of geological epochs, the evolution of life, and the early history of man vouchsafed by geology, paleontology, and archaeology."

J. Kagarlitski: "Reading Wells leaves one with mixed feelings. Sometimes one is exasperated by the didactic, by the unfinished nature of the story and by the way he jumps from one subject to another. All his life Wells tried to write the naked truth about his heroes and himself and there is no need to conceal the fact that he did not always show ordinary, political or literary tact. But he was a great prophet and the grand daredevil of modern literature. One cannot judge his worth unless one adopts the same great scale that he adopted in literature and in life."

Robert Lowndes: "None of Wells's fictional efforts are simply stories and nothing more; all are vehicles for his insights upon the human condition, criticism of existing social conditions, and propaganda for the scientifically run society he envisioned as possible for the world . . . . [However,] Wells died in 1946, no longer a voice to which the world listened eagerly, and many of what he considered his most important works are forgotten."

FURTHER READING

BIBLIOGRAPHICAL GUIDE

PAPERBACK EDITIONS

The Time Machine. New York: Pyramid Books, 1966.

The Invisible Man/The War of the Worlds. New York: Washington Square Press, 1962. Introduction by Arthur C. Clarke.

The Invisible Man. New York: Scholastic Library Edition, 1963. Afterword by George Bennett.

Tono-Bungay. New York: New American Library of Dodd, Mead & Co., 1960. Introduction by Harry T. Moore.

CRITICAL AND BIOGRAPHICAL WORKS ON H. G. WELLS

Belgion, Montgomery. *H. G. Wells.* London: Longmans, Green and Co., 1953. Reprinted 1964 with bibliographical additions. (Writers and Their Work, #40).

Bergonzi, Bernard. *The Early Wells: A Study of the Scientific Romances.* Toronto: University of Toronto Press, 1961.

Costa, Richard Haven. *H. G. Wells.* New York: Twayne, 1967. (Twayne's English Authors Series, #43).

Hillegas, Mark R. *The Future as Nightmare: H. G. Wells and the Anti-Utopians.* New York: Oxford University Press, 1967.

Ingvald, Raknem. *H. G. Wells and His Critics*. Oslo: 1962. New York: Hillary House.

Kagarlitski, J. *The Life and Thought of H. G. Wells*. New York: Barnes & Noble, Inc. Translated from the Russian by Moura Budberg.

Vallentin, Antonina. *H. G. Wells: Prophet of Our Day*. New York: The John Day Co., 1950. Translated from the French by Daphne Woodward.

Wagar, W. Warren. *H. G. Wells and the World State*. New Haven: Yale University Press, 1961.

Ward, A. C. *Twentieth-Century English Literature, 1901 – 1960*. London: Methuen. New York: Barnes & Noble, Inc., 1964 (Thirteenth Edition). pp. 25–34.

NOTES

MONARCH® *NOTES* *AND STUDY GUIDES*

ARE AVAILABLE AT RETAIL STORES EVERYWHERE

In the event your local bookseller
cannot provide you with other
Monarch titles you want —

ORDER ON THE FORM BELOW:

Complete order form appears
on inside front & back covers
for your convenience.

Simply send retail price, local
sales tax, if any, plus 35¢ per
book to cover mailing and
handling.

TITLE #	AUTHOR & TITLE (exactly as shown on title listing)	PRICE
	PLUS ADDITIONAL 35¢ PER BOOK FOR POSTAGE	
	GRAND TOTAL	$

MONARCH® **PRESS, a Simon & Schuster Division of Gulf & Western Corporation**
Mail Service Department, 1230 Avenue of the Americas, New York, N.Y. 10020

I enclose $ .... to cover retail price, local sales tax, plus mailing
and handling.

Name _____
(Please print)
Address _____

City _____ State _____ Zip _____

Please send check or money order. We cannot be responsible for cash.